MW00991403

THE ROLLING STONES TRIVIA BOOK

Uncover The Epic History & Facts Every
Fan Should Know!

By Dale Raynes

Bridge Press

dp@purplelink.org

Please consider writing a review!

Just visit: purplelink.org/review

Copyright 2021. Dale Raynes. All Rights Reserved.

No part of this book may be reproduced or transmitted in any form or by any means, electronic or mechanical, including photocopying, recording or by any other form without written permission from the publisher.

ISBN: 978-1-955149-07-5

TABLE OF CONTENTS:

THE ROLLING STONES

As soon as you hear their name, you know them. The raw sexuality in Mick Jagger's voice, the ramshackle immediacy of Keith Richards riffs, and the understated, but always perfect, rhythm section all create the inimitable signature sound of the Rolling Stones. In their prime, the original bad boys of rock were seemingly always in trouble for some form of sex or drug-related antics. They played a crucial role in the culture of the 1960s, playing devil's advocate to the cleaner image of their friendly British rivals, the Beatles. The Rolling Stones embodied rock both in sound and image, launching countless imitators and writing some of the most unforgettable rock tunes along the way.

Today, the Rolling Stones are renowned for their longevity. With 52 years between their first album and their latest, this group of London lads is now a respected institution. However, what is often forgotten in their notoriety is the sheer quality of their music. The string of albums they put together, from *Aftermath* in 1965 to *Exile on Main Street* in 1972, is as good as those produced by any other artist in history. Possibly better! Though they never recovered the musical majesty of their prime, the Stones haven't released a stinker in five decades of recording.

In sum, the Rolling Stones have presented an irresistible combination of quality and iconic imagery for over half a century. To know the Stones is to know the history and imagery of rock'n'roll. So, how much do you know about their unique journey from rebellious blues-loving lads to respectable multi-millionaires? Only one way to find out.

CHAPTER 1:

THE ROOTS OF
THE ROLLING STONES

1. Where did Keith Richards grow up?
    a. Scotland
    b. The City of London
    c. Birmingham
    d. Kent

2. In the legendary meeting where Mick Jagger and Keith Richards decided to cooperate musically, Jagger held what under his arm?
    a. Pictures of pretty girls
    b. Cigarettes
    c. Old blues records
    d. A guitar

3. Did Mick Jagger and Keith Richards know each other before that meeting?
    a. Yes, from school
    b. Yes, they had heard each other play
    c. Yes, from music classes
    d. No, it was their first meeting

4. When Mick Jagger started working with Keith Richards, what was his primary occupation?
    a. Student at the London School of Economics

    b. Singer for another band

    c. Worked at a tobacco shop

    d. A banker at Barclays Bank

5. Why did multi-instrumentalist, and original band member, Brian Jones drop out of high school?

    a. To form a band

    b. Problems with the law

    c. He impregnated a girl

    d. His terrible grades

6. What was the name of the first band Richards and Jagger played in together?

    a. Blues Boys

    b. Bluesbreakers

    c. They were always called the Rolling Stones

    d. Blues Incorporated

7. Which original member was initially a jazz musician?

    a. Bill Wyman

    b. Brian Jones

    c. Keith Richards

    d. Charlie Watts

8. The name the Rolling Stones was inspired by whom?

    a. Muddy Waters

    b. Elvis

    c. A well-known magazine

    d. Bo Diddley

9. How many members did the Stones have in their original line-up?

    a. Four

b. Five

c. Six

d. Seven

10. Where did the band play their first show?

   a. The Troubadour

   b. The Marquee

   c. The Cavern

   d. The 100 Club

11. Why couldn't the first manager of the Stones, Andrew Loog Oldham, register officially as their representative?

   a. He was too young

   b. His criminal record

   c. He was a bigamist

   d. Because the Stones had a bad reputation

12. What image did Andrew Loog Oldham cultivate in the band?

   a. Suits and ties like the Beatles

   b. Slicked, back hair and leather jackets

   c. Sharply dressed pretty boys

   d. Animalistic and scruffy outfits

13. Why did Decca Records give the Stones a particularly generous deal for their first recording contract?

   a. They impressed the record company

   b. Oldham's negotiation skills

   c. They regretted passing on the Beatles

   d. Decca was rich at that time

14. What was the first single released by the Rolling Stones?

   a. Come On

b. Not Fade Away

c. You Better Move On

d. Route 66

15. What was the status of the Rolling Stones in their first UK nationwide tour?

    a. They headlined the tour supported by Bo Diddley

    b. Bo Diddley headlined, and they supported

    c. They were co-headliners with the Beatles

    d. They opened for the Beatles

16. Who wrote the second single released by the band?

    a. Jagger-Richards

    b. Lennon-McCartney

    c. Muddy Waters

    d. Chuck Berry

17. The Stones' third single was "Not Fade Away," which was originally a Buddy Holly song. However, many critics pointed out that it sounded exactly like what other artists?

    a. The Beatles

    b. Elvis

    c. Bo Diddley

    d. Muddy Waters

18. Manager Oldham told his band that they would make no money until they wrote their own songs and pressured them to get as many as possible for their first album. How many original songs appeared on their first album?

    a. None

    b. One

    c. Two

d. Three

19. What was the first #1 hit the band scored in the UK?

    a. "Not Fade Away"
    b. "(I Can't Get No) Satisfaction"
    c. "Time is on My Side"
    d. "It's All Over Now"

20. In June 1964, the Rolling Stones conducted their first US tour. How many top 20 hits had they had in the country at that point?

    a. None
    b. One
    c. Two
    d. Three

ANSWERS

1. D- Kent

2. C- Old blues records

3. A- Yes, from school

4. A- Student at the London School of Economics

5. C- He impregnated a girl

6. A- Blues Boys

7. D- Charlies Watts

8. A- Muddy Waters

9. C- Six

10. B- The Marquee

11. A- He was too young

12. D- Animalistic and scruffy outfits

13. C- They regretted passing on the Beatles

14. A- Come On

15. B- Bod Diddley headlined, and they supported

16. B- Lennon-McCartney

17. C- Bo Diddley

18. B- One

19. D- "It's All Over Now"

20. A- None

DID YOU KNOW?

- Jagger and Richards were in the same class as children and were quite good friends. However, they lost touch after the Jagger family moved away. Music brought them together again and created one of the longest-lasting creative partnerships in rock history.

- British blues musician Alexis Korner played a significant role in putting the Rolling Stones together. His band Blues Incorporated included Charlies Watts and Brian Jones. In fact, that is how the band met Brian Jones. Korner introduced Jones to Richards and Jagger at the Ealing Jazz Club. He also played an instrumental role in introducing and inspiring other top British blues bands such as Cream and Free.

- I think we can all agree that the Rolling Stones is a far better name than Blues Boys or Blues Incorporated. But how and when did they switch? Everyone in the band thought the existing names were not very good. When Brian Jones was interviewed by Jazz News magazine, the reporter asked the band's name. Jones saw a copy of the album *Best of Muddy Waters* and spontaneously replied "the Rollin' Stones" after one of the songs on the album. Needless to say, it stuck.

- The Rolling Stones sharpened their chops as a live band at the legendary Marquee Club on 90 Wardour Street, in the London neighborhood of Soho. The Rolling Stones had often frequented the club when it was still located on Oxford street and played their first show there in January 1963. As a tribute to the role it played in their development, the Stones went back and played a concert at the club in 1971. Unfortunately, the seminary rock club closed its doors for good in 2008.

- The Stones first played another famous London venue, the Crawdaddy, in February 1963. At this club, the band debuted the lineup that would achieve worldwide fame: Mick Jagger, Keith Richards, Brian Jones, Bill Wyman, and Charlies Watts. The crowds the Stones attracted were so big that the Crawdaddy granted them residency and moved to a larger venue. When the band moved on to bigger and greater things, the Crawdaddy replaced them with the enormously influential Yardbirds.

CHAPTER 2:

REACHING GLOBAL STARDOM

1. The band released its first LP album in the UK on April 16, 1964. What was it called?

    a. *England's Newest Hitmakers*
    b. *The Rolling Stones*
    c. *12 x 5*
    d. *The Rolling Stones, Now!*

2. When the Rolling Stones first toured Canada, the Canadian Broadcasting Corporation asked which provocative question?

    a. Why does anyone listen to the Rolling Stones?
    b. What is this noise they call the Rolling Stones?
    c. Should we let the Rolling Stones play in Canada?
    d. Would you let your daughter marry a Rolling Stone?

3. The band had a particular clause in their contract allowing them to record in any studio they wished to use. In which studio did they decide to record their debut album?

    a. Abbey Road Studios
    b. Regent Sound Studios
    c. Townhouse Studios
    d. Olympic Sound Studios

4. Which member of the "Rat Pack" mocked the band with eye-rolls and jokes about their hair when they came on his show in 1964?

    a. Frank Sinatra

b. Joey Bishop

c. Sammy Davis Jr.

d. Dean Martin

5. Did the Rolling Stones play the Ed Sullivan show when they visited the United States?

   a. Yes, on their first visit

   b. Yes, on their second visit

   c. Yes, but years after they were famous

   d. No, they never did

6. The Rolling Stones were so excited by their visit to 2120 South Michigan Avenue that they wrote a song about it. What is located at that address?

   a. Chuck Berry's house

   b. Chess Records

   c. The Apollo Theater

   d. Sun Records

7. In their single "Little Red Rooster," they ask that if you see the rooster in question, you do what?

   a. Keep him safe

   b. Don't cook him

   c. Drive him home

   d. Look away

8. Jagger and Richards were not confident about their songwriting abilities. Which song did Richards say gave him the confidence to believe in his composing skills?

   a. "You Better Move On"

   b. "I Just Wanna Make Love to You"

   c. "It's All Over Now"

d. "The Last Time"

9. Which early Stones classic confused American fans by referring knowingly to several London neighborhoods?

   a. "Play with Fire"
   b. "Mother's Little Helper"
   c. "Ruby Tuesday"
   d. "Heart of Stone"

10. The legendary riff from "(I Can't Get No) Satisfaction" was so influential that music stores almost immediately ran out of the pedal Richards used to play it. What effect was it?

    a. Sola Sound Tone Bender
    b. Electro Harmonix LBP-1
    c. Arbiter Fuzz Face
    d. Maestro FZ-1 Fuzz-Tone

11. Many Stones songs seem quite misogynistic in retrospect. Which early song was so problematic that feminists have written books and articles about it?

    a. "Little Red Rooster"
    b. "Under My Thumb"
    c. "(I Can't Get No) Satisfaction"
    d. "Let's Spend the Night Together"

12. The Stones scored their second massive international hit with "Get Off of My Cloud." What was it about?

    a. Drugs
    b. Annoying neighbors
    c. Sex
    d. The pressure to get another hit

13. On the album *Aftermath*, Brian Jones blossomed and played a variety of unorthodox instruments. What did he play on the song "Lady Jane?"

    a. A harp

    b. A harpsichord

    c. The dulcimer

    d. An accordion

14. Before he focused on other instruments, Brian Jones was primarily a guitarist. What unusual guitar was he associated with?

    a. A white teardrop-shaped Vox

    b. A V-necked Fender

    c. A double-necked Gibson

    d. The Domino Californian

15. Which Stones classic was unjustifiably called a Beatles rip-off because it included a sitar part?

    a. "Have You Seen Your Mother, Baby, Standing in the Shadows?"

    b. "19th Nervous Breakdown"

    c. "Paint it Black"

    d. "Mothers Little Helper"

16. Where did the Rolling Stones record their classic album *Aftermath*?

    a. London

    b. New York

    c. Los Angeles

    d. Paris

17. Brian Jones was dating the sophisticated model Anita Pallenberg during his musical prime. How did his bandmates react to her?

   a. Jagger fell in love with her, and Richards hated her
   b. Richards fell in love with her, and Jagger slept with her
   c. Jagger was jealous of their relationship; Richards fell in love with her
   d. Jagger and Richards became good friends with her

18. The Stones loved the Regent Sound Studio. What did the engineers there use to create better acoustics?

   a. Egg cartons on the ceiling
   b. Cardboard tubes for the microphones
   c. Tinfoil on the walls
   d. The drums were kept on the roof

19. Which Quentin Tarantino movie featured a cover of the *Aftermath* cut "Out of Time" in its entirety?

   a. *Reservoir Dogs*
   b. *Pulp Fiction*
   c. *Kill Bill*
   d. *Once Upon a Time in Hollywood*

20. Who had the most commercially successful version of "Out of Time?"

   a. The Rolling Stones
   b. Chris Farlowe
   c. The Ramones
   d. The Bee Gees

ANSWERS

1. B- *The Rolling Stones*

2. D- Would you let your daughter marry a Rolling Stone?

3. B- Regent Sound Studios

4. D- Dean Martin

5. B- Yes, on their second visit

6. B- Chess Records

7. C- Drive him home

8. D- "The Last Time"

9. A- "Play with Fire"

10. D- Maestro FZ-1 Fuzz-Tone

11. B- Under My Thumb

12. D- The pressure to get another hit

13. C- The dulcimer

14. A- A white teardrop-shaped Vox

15. C- "Paint It Black"

16. C- Los Angeles

17. C- Jagger was jealous of their relationship; Richards fell in love with her

18. A- Egg cartons on the ceiling

19. D- *Once Upon a Time in Hollywood*

20. B- Chris Farlowe

DID YOU KNOW?

- "(I Can't Get No) Satisfaction" was one of the biggest hits of the 1960s and saw the Stones become one of the world's biggest acts. However, it could have been a very different song. The famous riff was supposed to be played by a horn section. Keith played the distorted opening part as a placeholder to denote what the horns would be doing. The rest of the band insisted that they keep the riff, even though Richards objected. The results set the standard for song openings for years to come.

- Rather than credit all band members for group-penned compositions; the band came up with a strange pseudonym. Those songs were credited as written by Nanker Phelge. Bassist Bill Wyman explained that "Phelge came from Edith Grove's flatmate Jimmy Phelge, while a Nanker was a revolting face that band members, Brian, in particular, would pull." All of the members shared royalties on the Nanker Phege numbers, including 2120 South Michigan Avenue and Play with Fire.

- The band did not want to call their brilliant 1966 album *Aftermath*. Instead, Andrew Loog Oldham wished to call the album "Could you Walk on the Water" and accompany it with a picture of the band performing that miraculous feat. However, Decca was concerned about an adverse reaction from Christians worldwide, and they vetoed the idea. The unhappy band settled on *Aftermath* instead.

- *Aftermath* was a turning point for the Stones and rock music in general. After years of performing covers, Richards and Jagger finally took the leap and wrote an entire album's worth of material. Mick recalled later the significance of the move and told *Rolling Stone* magazine that with this album, the Stones "finally laid to rest the ghost of having to do these very nice and interesting, no doubt, but still, cover versions of old R&B songs–which we didn't really feel we were doing justice, to be perfectly honest." The result was a dark masterpiece.

- During a show in Sacramento in 1965, Keith almost died. The guitarist received a massive electric shock from a microphone that was not correctly tethered. Richards did not move for seven minutes as an ambulance rushed over. A doctor at the hospital told Keith that the thick rubber soles of his new Hush Puppies suede boots probably saved his life.

CHAPTER 3:

FROM THE SUMMER OF LOVE TO ALTAMONT

1. The Stones fans proved incredibly unruly at their Royal Albert Hall concert of September 23, 1966. What happened as a result of that show?

    a. They burned down the venue
    b. Rock bands were banned from it
    c. Hundreds were arrested
    d. The seats were torn out

2. When recording *Got Live if You Want It,* the crowd noise was a significant problem for engineer Glyn Johns. Where did he place the microphones to get the best results?

    a. Under the stage
    b. Near the amplifiers
    c. On the roof
    d. On the balconies

3. Which member of the band is so famously cheap that he has been known to pocket the money intended for a tip before leaving restaurants?

    a. Mick Jagger
    b. Keith Richards
    c. Brian Jones
    d. Charlie Watts

4. According to his memoirs, which Rolling Stone slept with 278 women in the first two years after the band achieved global fame?

   a. Mick Jagger
   b. Bill Wyman
   c. Keith Richards
   d. Brian Jones

5. How did manager Andrew Loog Oldham react when Jagger and Richards were charged with drug possession in 1967?

   a. He gave a controversial press conference
   b. He turned himself into the police
   c. He fled the country
   d. He was the one who tipped of the police

6. What was the last album the Stones recorded with Andrew Loog Oldham as manager and producer?

   a. *Got Live if You Want It*
   b. *Aftermath*
   c. *December's Children*
   d. *Between the Buttons*

7. LAPD officers showed up at RCA studios when the band recorded their hit single "Let's Spend the Night Together." What did they do?

   a. Arrested band members
   b. Told them to stop because it was late
   c. Smoked weed with the band
   d. Let them use their truncheons for a sound effect

8. Which member of a future legendary band wrote the string arrangements for the band's 1967 album *Their Satanic Majesties Request*?

   a. John Paul Jones of Led Zeppelin
   b. Keith Emerson of Emerson Lake and Palmer
   c. Robert Fripp of King Crimson
   d. Alan Parsons of the Alan Parsons Project

9. In 1967, the *News of the World* published a story about Mick Jagger popping Benzedrine tablets and walking around with a big block of hashish. Was the story true?

   a. They made it up
   b. It was all true
   c. It was Brian Jones
   d. They got it from a wrong source

10. Which Rolling Stones album was criticized at the time with accusations that it was a cheap knock-off of the Beatles classic *Sgt. Pepper's Lonely Hearts Club Band*?

   a. *Between the Buttons*
   b. *Their Satanic Majesties Request*
   c. *Let it Bleed*
   d. *Beggars Banquet*

11. Which classic Stones song was recorded during the sessions for *Beggars Banquet* but not released on the album?

   a. "Street Fighting Man"
   b. "Sympathy for the Devil"
   c. "Jumpin' Jack Flash"
   d. "You Can't Always Get What You Want"

12. "In Another Land" was the first Stones single sung by a non-Jagger member of the band. Who sang and wrote the minor hit?

   a. Keith Richards
   b. Bill Wyman
   c. Charlie Watts
   d. Brian Jones

13. Which historical event is NOT blamed on the Devil in the song "Sympathy for the Devil?"

   a. The assassination of Lincoln
   b. The Russian Revolution
   c. The Nazi blitzkrieg invasions
   d. The crucifixion of Jesus

14. Gifted blues guitarist Mick Taylor replaced Brian Jones in 1969. Which classic John Mayall album established Taylor's reputation?

   a. A Hard Road
   b. Crusade
   c. Empty Rooms
   d. The Turning Point

15. Which song did the Stones debut at Hyde Park's concert, which they performed two days after Brian Jones's death?

   a. "Jumpin' Jack Flash"
   b. "You Can't Always Get What You Want"
   c. "Brown Sugar"
   d. "Honky Tonk Woman"

16. The first song on *Let it Bleed* was "Gimme Shelter." The background vocal performance by Merry Clayton is

considered one of the finest of all time. What do some people credit with the unique sound she achieved on the cut?

    a. She was stoned

    b. She was pregnant

    c. She had just had sex

    d. She smoked a lot

17. The album *Let It Bleed* was recorded around the time Jones was fired from the band. Did Brian Jones or Mick Taylor play on it?

    a. Mick Taylor did

    b. Brian Jones did

    c. Neither did

    d. Both did

18. Which song from this era did Donald Trump like to play during campaign rallies in 2016?

    a. "You Can't Always Get What You Want"

    b. "Gimme Shelter"

    c. "Street Fighting Man"

    d. "Honky Tonk Woman"

19. At Altamont, California, the Rolling Stones show ended in disaster when concert-goer Meredith Hunter was murdered. Who killed him?

    a. The police

    b. Drugged-out fans

    c. Rolling Stones roadies

    d. Hells Angels bikers

20. What song was the band playing as Hunter was stabbed repeatedly?

a. "Sympathy for the Devil"
b. "(I Can't Get No) Satisfaction"
c. "Under My Thumb"
d. "Let's Spend the Night Together"

ANSWERS

1. B- Rock bands were banned from it

2. D- On the balconies

3. A- Mick Jagger. Yup. Even after he was a millionaire.

4. B- Bill Wyman. He claims Jagger was with 30 and Keith a mere six

5. C- He fled the country

6. D- *Between the Buttons*

7. D- Let them use their truncheons for a sound effect.

8. A- John Paul Jones of Led Zeppelin

9. C- It was Brian Jones

10. B- *Their Satanic Majesties Request*. However, critics view it far more today

11. C- "Jumpin' Jack Flash"

12. B- Bill Wyman

13. A- The assassination of Lincoln, but he is blamed for the death of President Kennedy and his brother Bobby

14. B- Crusade

15. D- "Honky Tonk Woman"

16. B- She was pregnant

17. D- Both did. Both played on two separate songs.

18. A- "You Can't Always Get What You Want"

19. D- Hells Angels Bikers

20. C- "Under My Thumb"

DID YOU KNOW?

- In 1967, the band went on a trip to Morocco with Jones' girlfriend Anita Pallenberg and Jagger's significant other, Marianne Faithful. However, Jones got sick on the way and remained in the French city of Toulouse. Richards and Pallenberg went on without him, and he spent his 25th birthday ill and alone in France. Richards and Pallenberg ended up together and began an affair that lasted for 12 years. The rift between Jones and the rest of the band became irreparable at that point. As Richards later admitted, "That was the final nail in the coffin with me and Brian. He'd never forgive me for that, and I don't blame him, but hell, shit happens."

- Jagger and Richards were both charged with drug possession in 1967. Jaggers was sentenced to three months in jail. The London Times released a famous editorial titled "Who Breaks a Butterfly Upon a Wheel?" where they charged the police with mistreating the band. The band responded with a tongue-in-cheek single called "We Love You," where you could hear jail doors slamming closed. Following an appeal, the verdict concerning Richards was overturned, and Jagger's sentence was reduced to a conditional discharge.

- The album *Their Satanic Majesties* was the first produced by the band. The trouble was that they had little idea what they were doing and members were consuming large amounts of drugs at the time. As a result, the sessions were chaotic. Jagger later lamented the results: "There's a lot of rubbish on *Satanic Majesties*. Just too much time on our hands, too many drugs, no producer to tell us, 'Enough already, thank you very much, now can we just get on with this song?' Anyone let loose in the studio will produce stuff like that. There was simply too much hanging around. It's like believing everything you do is great and not having any editing." Still, the album has moments of brilliance, especially the epic song "2000 Light Years from Home."

- In 1968, the Rolling Stones recorded an expensive spectacle called *The Rolling Stones Rock and Roll Circus*. It included some of the biggest names in music, including Eric Clapton, John Lennon, and the Who. The loose concept behind it was that the band's performances would approximate a traditional English circus show. However, the special was never released for two reasons. First, the Stones were unhappy with their performance, which they deemed substandard. They were reportedly wholly upstaged by the Who. Second, it was their last performance with Brian Jones, who died soon after. Ian Anderson, of Jethro Tull, remembered that "Brian Jones was well past his sell-by date by then… We spoke to Brian, and he didn't know what was going on. He was rather cut off from the others–there was a lot of embarrassed silence. But a delightful chap, and we felt rather sorry for him."

- On June 8, 1969, Brian Jones was fired from the Rolling Stones. Less than a month later, he was found dead in his home's swimming pool at Cotchford Farm, the site where A.A. Milne wrote the *Winnie-the-Pooh* books. Some people believe the death was suspicious and that foul play was involved. Brian was the first of the unfortunate "27 club" of rock legends who died at age 27. It later included Jimi Hendrix, Jim Morrison, Janis Joplin, Kurt Cobain, and Amy

Winehouse. The band went on with a free concert at Hyde Park scheduled for two days after his death.

CHAPTER 4:

THE GREATEST ROCK'N'ROLL BAND IN THE WORLD

1. Why did the Rolling Stones follow *Let it Bleed* with *Get Yer Ya-Ya's Out!*, their second live album?

    a. Their shows at the time were excellent
    b. They thought the first live album was bad
    c. They were sick of bootlegs making money off them
    d. They were contractually obligated

2. Was *Get Yer Ya-Ya's Out!* fully recorded live and in concert?

    a. Yes, warts and all
    b. Yes, but with heavy mixing and studio overdubs
    c. No, some songs were recorded in the studio
    d. No, almost all of it was recorded in the studio

3. Where was the cover of that live album photographed?

    a. The French Riviera
    b. In the bathroom of a bar
    c. On a highway near Birmingham
    d. On an English farm

4. The album *Sticky Fingers* was the first to feature what?

    a. The iconic tongue and lips logo
    b. Guitar by Mick Taylor
    c. A Keith Richards vocal
    d. Several curse words

5. Which of these is not a subject addressed in the song "Brown Sugar?"

   a. Slavery
   b. Cocaine
   c. Cunnilingus
   d. Sadomasochism

6. How many songs on *Sticky Fingers* was Mick Taylor credited with writing?

   a. None
   b. One
   c. Two
   d. Three

7. Mick Jagger asked the designer of the iconic tongue and lips symbol to make his tongue look like what?

   a. He was licking ice cream
   b. He was engaged in oral sex
   c. The Hindu goddess Kali
   d. The tongue of Gene Simmons

8. The band had a mobile recording studio built for them to record wherever they wanted. Which classic rock staple mentions it by name?

   a. "Hotel California" by the Eagles
   b. "Whole Lotta Love" by Led Zeppelin
   c. "Rocket Man" by Elton John
   d. "Smoke on the Water" by Deep Purple

9. After recording *Sticky Fingers*, the band discovered that their management had not paid taxes. How many years of back payments did they owe the British government?

a. Seven years
b. Six years
c. Five years
d. Four years

10. What percentage of their earnings were the Stones expected to pay when they went on tax exile in 1971?

    a. 63%
    b. 73%
    c. 83%
    d. 93%

11. What area of the world did the Stones choose as their tax shelter to avoid paying their back taxes?

    a. Brazil
    b. Southern France
    c. The Bahamas
    d. New York

12. When did the band resolve their tax problems with the British government?

    a. In the 70s
    b. In the 80s
    c. In the 90s
    d. They never did

13. While recording the seminal album *Exile on Main Street*, Keith Richards began to blow off recording dates. Why did he do this?

    a. He discovered heroin
    b. He had a new girlfriend
    c. He wasn't getting along with the band

d. He hated the music

14. Keith Richards and country-rock genius Gram Parsons became fast friends at what landmark location?

    a. Alcatraz island
    b. Stonehenge monument
    c. The ruins of Machu Picchu
    d. Notre Dame Cathedral

15. The posters for the Stones concert movie *Ladies and Gentlemen: The Rolling Stones* described the sound system used for the move as what?

    a. Phantasmagorical
    b. Beauterrific
    c. Quadrasound
    d. Intra-surround-experience

16. A 2006 book on the making of *Exile on Mainstreet* is titled what?

    a. Exile on Main Street: Sex, Drugs, and Maybe Some Rock'n'roll
    b. Exile on Main Street: A Season in Hell with the Rolling Stones
    c. Exile on Main Street: The Story of a Classic
    d. Exile on Main Street: Heroines of Heroin

17. What was Bill Wyman's main complaint about the process of recording *Exile on Main Street*?

    a. The excessive drugs
    b. Fighting in the band
    c. It was hard to get English food
    d. The sound mix was poor

18. Charlie Watts was known as the reserved and in control Stone. However, during the recording of *Exile*, he was over-indulging in what?

    a. Marijuana
    b. Gambling
    c. Cocaine
    d. Brandy

19. Was the follow-up to *Exile on Main Street*, *Goat's Head Soup*, as successful as its predecessor?

    a. It was similarly successful
    b. It also reached No. 1 but was panned by critics
    c. It didn't succeed commercially or critically
    d. It didn't sell but is considered a classic

20. True or False: There is a documentary about the *Exile on Main Street* tour called *Cocksucker Blues*?

ANSWERS

1. C- They were sick of bootlegs making money off them

2. B- Yes, but with heavy mixing and studio overdubs

3. C- On a highway near Birmingham

4. A- The iconic tongue and lips logo

5. B- Cocaine

6. A- None. However, Taylor has claimed that he played a significant part in writing "Sway" and "Moonlight Mile."

7. C- The Hindu goddess Kali

8. D- "Smoke on the Water" by Deep Purple

9. A- Seven years

10. D- 93%

11. B- Southern France

12. D- They never did

13. A- He discovered heroin

14. B- Stonehenge monument

15. C- Quadrasound

16. B- Exile on Main Street: A Season in Hell with the Rolling Stones

17. C- It was hard to get English food

18. D- Brandy

19. C- It also reached No. 1 but was panned by critics

20. True. The movie remains unreleased but not because of its name. The band thought too much of it made them look bad.

DID YOU KNOW?

- The cover of *Sticky Fingers* was designed by Andy Warhol, one of the most famous post-war era artists. It featured the bottom half of a jeans-clad man. It included a functioning zipper, which, when opened, revealed a pair of underwear. The words "This Is Not Etc." were printed on the undergarments. The elaborate design sometimes damaged the record. In Spain, the cover was replaced with a less controversial cover.

- *Sticky Fingers* was the first album released on the Rolling Stone's own record label 'Rolling Stones Records.' When the label was in operation, they used several large record companies such as Atlantic and EMI to distribute their records. Unlike some of their contemporaries who formed record contracts (the Beatles and Led Zeppelin), they did not try to sign other acts. The company was primarily a vehicle for Stones records. Rolling Stones Records was dissolved when the band signed with Virgin Records in 1992.

- *Exile on Main Street* is generally considered the greatest Rolling Stones album of all time. It was also the peak of Richards' influence on their direction, in the sense that the musical style was the loose and gritty blues-rock, which he favored. Perhaps because of this, Jagger has always expressed reservations about the quality of the album. Although it has good moments, the singer has said that the production made it sound "lousy," and it lacked focus. Singer Tom Waits expressed what most of us think of it, referring to it as a "tree of life." In the opinion of many fans and critics, they would never make an album of that quality again.

- The Rolling Stones Mobile Studio doesn't look like much, but some of the best rock of the 1970s was recorded there. The Stones recorded parts of both *Sticky Fingers* and *Exile on Main Street* within the unit. Meanwhile, Led Zeppelin recorded their *III* and *IV* elements there and the Who used it for *Who's Next*. Acts as diverse as Bob Marley, Dire Straits, the Ramones, and Iron Maiden recorded work in the studio. Today it can be found at the National Music Centre in Calgary, Alberta.

- The biggest hit off the album *Goat's Head Soup* was the single "Angie." The song addressed a painful breakup in a particularly evocative way. Therefore, there has been a great deal of speculation over who the song is about. Though both Jagger and Richards deny it was about anyone specific, there has long been speculation that it is either about David Bowie's first wife Angie Bowie or Jagger's breakup with Marianne Faithful.

CHAPTER 5:

THE STONES LOST YEARS

1. What was the main problem the Stones faced when they toured in support of the *Goat's Head Soup* album?

    a. Problems with Bianca Jagger
    b. Richards' drug problem
    c. Mick Taylor wasn't getting along with the band
    d. They were banned from several countries for drugs and tax issues

2. Where did the band record *Goat's Head Soup*?

    a. The Bahamas
    b. Tahiti
    c. Jamaica
    d. The Maldives

3. Which legendary guitarist cut a track with the Stones on the *Goat's Head Soup* sessions, one which was not included on the album?

    a. Jeff Beck
    b. Jimmy Page
    c. Eric Clapton
    d. Rory Gallagher

4. When Mick Taylor left the band, the Stones considered some amazing lead guitarists before hiring Ronnie Wood. Who amongst these individuals was NOT considered?

    a. Jeff Beck

b. Joe Walsh

c. Peter Frampton

d. Rory Gallagher

5. Which of these guitarists did NOT play on the first album to follow Mick Taylor's departure?

   a. Ronnie Wood

   b. Harvey Mandel

   c. Wayne Perkins

   d. Clem Clempson

6. What did critics think of Ronnie Wood's previous band, the Faces, compared to the Stones?

   a. That they were better than the Stones

   b. That they were of similar quality to the Stones

   c. That they were a pale imitation of the Stones

   d. That they were very different from the Stones

7. When Ronnie Wood took up the Stones on their job offer in 1975, what was his employment status?

   a. Full member of the Stones

   b. Full member of the Stones and the Faces

   c. Salaried employee of the Stones

   d. Session musician for the Stones

8. When the Stones launched their first North American tour with Ronnie Wood, they only included one pre-1968 song in their setlist. What was it?

   a. "Get Off of My Cloud"

   b. "(I Can't Get No) Satisfaction"

   c. "Paint it Black"

   d. "Let's Spend the Night Together"

9. Richards and Jagger could not agree on which songs to include on the double *Love You Live* album. How was the problem resolved?

   a. Richards got what he wanted
   b. Jagger got what he wanted
   c. They learned to cooperate
   d. They each chose the songs on one record

10. Richards' two-month-old son died while on tour in Europe. What did the guitarist do the night he found out?

   a. Left without telling the band members
   b. Asked to cancel the show
   c. Asked to cancel the tour
   d. Played the show anyway

11. When the Stones toured Canada in 1977, Richards and his wife Pallenberg were arrested for the possession of heroin. After a protracted legal battle, what sentence was Richards given?

   a. A million-dollar fine
   b. 500 hours of community service
   c. To play two shows for charity
   d. A 10-year suspended sentence

12. Where did Jagger discover the talented harmonica player who contributed to the crossover disco hit "Miss You?"

   a. The Paris Metro
   b. A supermarket
   c. A blues club
   d. Studio 54

13. Having regained their popularity with the *Some Girls* album, the Stones were excited to open the fourth season of

Saturday Night Live as the musical guests. What number did they open with?

    a. "Miss You"
    b. "Beast of Burden"
    c. "Tumbling Dice"
    d. "Angie"

14. The Stones and the Sex Pistols had a very public feud. What did Jagger say about Sex Pistols singer Johnny Rotten?

    a. He lives with his mom
    b. He smells weird
    c. He can't sing
    d. He is ugly

15. How did the band end up settling their feud with the Sex Pistols?

    a. A fistfight
    b. A concert together
    c. Jagger paid Sid Vicious' legal fees
    d. Jagger played at Sid Vicious' funeral

16. The album *Some Girls* was a smash hit in the United States. How well did it sell in comparison to their older material in the country?

    a. It was one of their top five selling albums
    b. It was their third best-selling album
    c. It was their second best-selling album
    d. It was their best-selling album yet

17. The song "Some Girls "was the latest to attract controversy as possibly racist and misogynistic. However, Mick claimed

it was a parody of racist attitudes. According to the song, which group of girls "just want to get fucked all night"?

   a. White girls
   b. Chinese girls
   c. Indian girls
   d. Black girls

18. Did the Stones play the song "Some Girls" despite the controversy surrounding it?

   a. They never played it
   b. They never played it and apologized for it
   c. They played it in every show on the 1999 tour
   d. They rarely played it

19. The original cover of "Some Girls" included several female celebrities. Several of them (or their estates) were upset with the use. Which of these celebrities got a personal apology from Jagger?

   a. Farah Fawcett
   b. Liza Minelli
   c. Lucille Ball
   d. Raquel Welch

20. Due to its success, every song on *Some Girls* has been played live. Which two other Stones albums share the same distinction?

   a. *Let It Bleed and Sticky Fingers*
   b. *Exile on Mainstreet and Beggars Banquet*
   c. *Aftermath and December's Children*
   d. *Tattoo You and Goat's Head Soup*

ANSWERS

1. D- They were banned from several countries for drugs and tax issues

2. C- Jamaica

3. B- Jimmy Page

4. B- Joe Walsh

5. D- Clem Clempson

6. C- That they were a pale imitation of the Stones

7. C- Salaried employee of the Stones

8. A- Get Off of My Cloud

9. D- They each choose the songs on one record

10. D- Played the show anyway

11. C- To play two shows for charity

12. A- The Paris Metro

13. B- "Beast of Burden"

14. A- He lives with his mom

15. C- Jagger paid Sid Vicious' legal fees

16. D- It was their best-selling album yet

17. D- Black girls

18. C- They played it in every show on the 1999 tour

19. B- Liza Minelli

20. A- *Let It Bleed* and *Sticky Fingers*

DID YOU KNOW?

- Mick Taylor left the band in 1974 after the recording of "It's Only Rock'n'roll." The drugs and the lack of camaraderie in the band at that time were a factor, but perhaps the most frustrating for Taylor was that they treated him as a sideman and did not let him contribute material. In a 1980 interview, the gifted guitarist explained, "I was getting a bit fed up. I wanted to broaden my scope as a guitarist and do something else ... I wasn't really composing songs or writing at that time. I was just beginning to write, and that influenced my decision ... There are some people who can just ride along from crest to crest; they can ride along somebody else's success. And there are some people for whom that's not enough. It really wasn't enough for me."

- Jeff Beck is one of the best guitarists in the world, and the Stones have always deeply admired him. They considered him for the role when Brian Jones was fired, and they thought of Beck again when Taylor quit. The former Yardbirds guitarist was invited to jam with the Stones and soon realized it was an audition. However, he saw the band was in a chaotic state and decided to leave before this "audition" was over. Beck said about this experience that "some people might find it hard to believe that you'd walk away from the Stones gig, but Keith and I wouldn't have gone through an album without punching each other out anyway." It was probably a good idea since the next album the brilliant guitarist released was *Blow by Blow*, an absolute landmark of the jazz-fusion genre.

- The first Stones tour with Ronnie Wood was called Tour of the Americas. It was quite successful, but perhaps not their classiest moment. The band was trying to compete with the showy tours of contemporaries such as Kiss and Elton John. The enterprise was launched when they performed on a trailer pulled through Broadway. Also, the many stage props included a gigantic phallus. The phallus was affectionately known as "tired grandfather" because it did not always rise to the occasion.

- The cover of the *Love You Live* album was once again assigned to iconic artist Andy Warhol. The cover showed Jagger biting his hand for unknown reasons. The final cover has the band's and album's names scribbled on it, in Jagger's writing. Warhol was reportedly quite upset at the writing's addition, which he felt marred the visual effect.

- Aside from their legal troubles in Canada, the Stones caused a political scandal when they arrived in 1977. The prime minister's attractive young wife, Margaret Trudeau, spent the night of her sixth wedding anniversary partying with the band. She then disappeared to New York, sparking furious rumors that she was having an affair with Mick Jagger. Years later, Trudeau denied having sex with Jagger but lamented that "I should have slept with every single one of them."

CHAPTER 6:

START THEM UP – THE STONES IN THE '80S

1. In the late 1970s, Richards got off heroin. To what does he attribute his survival?

    a. His good genes
    b. Jagger's loyalty and support
    c. Sheer luck
    d. Only taking "top-quality shit"

2. What was Richards like during the recording sessions for *Emotional Rescue*?

    a. He was constantly lethargic and drunk
    b. He was hyperactive and coked up
    c. He was very professional
    d. He alternated between lethargic and hyperactive

3. What did the cover of the album *Emotional Rescue* feature?

    a. Naked pictures of the band
    b. X-rays of the band
    c. Heat emissions of the band
    d. Fingerprints of the band

4. The album *Tattoo You* was one of the biggest commercial successes in the bands' career and was well-received critically. How was it recorded?

a. The Stones set aside a good amount of time to work on it.
b. They banged it out in a few intense days.
c. The band was barely ever in the same room and relied on old outtakes.
d. Jagger and Richards did most of the work on their own.

5. The Stones had tried to play an early version of the rip-roaring hit single "Start Me Up" when recording *Some Girls*, but it didn't come together. What was the original version of the song?

   a. A slow reggae song
   b. A moving ballad
   c. A rootsy blues recording
   d. A four-on-the-floor disco number

6. What is the last line of the hit single "Start Me Up?"

   a. "You make a grown man cry"
   b. "You make a dead man come"
   c. "My palms are greasy"
   d. "I can't compete with the runners in the other heats"

7. Which jazz immortal played on the *Tattoo You* album?

   a. Miles Davis
   b. Sonny Rollins
   c. Chick Correa
   d. Thelonious Monk

8. During the Steel Wheel tour, Richards uncharacteristically refused to take the stage. Why?

   a. Someone drank his whisky
   b. Someone ate his shepherd's pie

c. Someone touched his guitar

d. He didn't feel like playing

9. In 1982, the band signed the biggest record contract of all time with which company?

    a. CBS

    b. Atlantic

    c. Columbia

    d. Virgin

10. The album *Undercover* featured a vintage nude model on its cover. What was covering her breasts?

    a. Hands

    b. Stickers

    c. Nothing

    d. Pins

11. 1What was the single "Undercover of the Night" about?

    a. Sex trafficking

    b. Corruption in South America

    c. The War on Drugs

    d. The Vietnam War

12. Why did MTV refuse to play the original version of the video for "Undercover of the Night?"

    a. The band wasn't fashionable

    b. The video wasn't good

    c. It was too sexual

    d. It was too violent

13. The band didn't love the song "Pretty Beat Up." What was their working name for it?

    a. Pile of dung

b. Dog crap

c. Garbage pile

d. Puke puddle

14. Which soul legend provided backing vocals on the song "One Hit (To the Body)?"

    a. Chaka Khan

    b. Curtis Mayfield

    c. Isaac Hayes

    d. Bobby Womack

15. Who played the guitar solo on "One Hit (To the Body)?"

    a. Keith Richards

    b. Ronnie Wood

    c. Mick Taylor

    d. Jimmy Page

16. The band almost broke up in the 1980s. What was the main cause of tensions in the band?

    a. Drugs

    b. Poor album sales

    c. Jagger's solo career

    d. Disagreement on the musical direction

17. What does Richards call the period where the band nearly broke up?

    a. "A damn shame"

    b. "World War III"

    c. "The lost days"

    d. "Mick's idiot days"

18. Who showed up to the sessions for the album *Dirty Work* straight out of rehab?

a. Bill Wyman
b. Charlie Watts
c. Ronnie Wood
d. Keith Richards

19. *Steel Wheels* was considered a significant return to form for the band. Where was it recorded?

a. Montserrat
b. Barbados
c. Sint Maarten
d. Saint Lucia

20. Throughout the 1980s, the Stones kept trying to release an old cut called "Claudine" but could not do so for fear of legal action. Who threatened to sue them if they released it?

a. Jagger's ex-girlfriend
b. A groupie they used to tour with
c. A murder suspect
d. A well-known author

ANSWERS

1. D- Only taking "top-quality shit"

2. D- He alternated between lethargic and hyperactive. He was substituting heroin with both cocaine and alcohol, and his mood shifted according to the substance recently consumed.

3. C- Heat emissions of the band

4. C- The band was barely ever in the same room and relied on old outtakes.

5. A - A slow reggae song

6. B- "You make a dead man come"

7. B- Sonny Rollins

8. B- Someone ate his shepherd's pie. He only took the stage after he was provided with another

9. A- CBS

10. Stickers. In the first edition, they were actual stickers that peeled off.

11. B- Corruption in South America

12. D- It was too violent

13. B- Dog crap-

14. D- Bobby Womack

15. D- Jimmy Page

16. C- Jagger's Solo Career

17. B- "World War III"

18. C- Ronnie Wood

19. A- Montserrat

20. C- A murder suspect. Claudine Longet was accused of murdering her boyfriend in 1976. However, in the end, she was only charged with a misdemeanour because key evidence was ruled inadmissible.

DID YOU KNOW?

- Some of *Tattoo You*'s tracks included Mick Taylor's graceful guitar work, but he was not credited for it. By this point, Taylor was sick of being marginalized by the band and demanded a share of the royalties, or he would pursue legal action. He was eventually given the royalties he deserved.

- Part of the massive contract the Stones signed with CBS was hidden from (most of) the band. CBS Records President Walter Yetnikoff gave Jagger a large solo deal. Yetnikoff believed that the Stone's best days were behind them, and Jagger could be one of the biggest solo stars of the 80s. This caused a rift that almost destroyed the band, as Jagger cancelled tours and postponed recording sessions to focus on his two mid-decade solo albums. Jagger also used all his albums' material, arriving for recording sessions with no new songs. If Jagger's solo albums had been more successful, there is an excellent chance the Stones would have broken up.

- The bitterness between Jagger and Richards in the mid-80s is the subject of several songs from the time. For example, in the song "Had it With You," Richards accuses the singer of "Serving out injunctions / Shouting out instructions / But I had it I had it I had it with you." Meanwhile, in "Dirty Work," he says of Jagger, "Living high, sitting in the sun / Sit on your ass till your work is done." However, the complexity of his feelings for Jagger is also evident. In "Had It With You," Richards also remembers that "I love you with a passion / In and out of fashion / Always got behind you / When others tried to blind you." In the end, Richards' love for Jagger won out. Indeed, Richards later said his relationship with the singer is similar to a married couple staying together because of the kids and the life they built together.

- The album *Steel Wheels* saw the Stones put the rocky period behind them. Before leaving home for the recording sessions, Richards told his wife he would be back in two weeks or 48 hours, depending on how things went. He ended up staying. The resulting album was seen as a significant return to form, although today, critics believe it was overrated. However, the camaraderie was reestablished for good. Although Bill Wyman would soon leave the band, they would never come that close to breaking up again.

CHAPTER 7:

THE STONES IN THE '90S

1. Bill Wyman formally left the band in 1993. What was his last album with the band?

   a. *Voodoo Lounge*
   b. *Undercover*
   c. *Dirty Work*
   d. *Steel Wheels*

2. The Stones had the highest-grossing tour of the 1990s. Which tour was it?

   a. A Bigger Bang
   b. Bridges to Babylon
   c. Voodoo Lounge
   d. Steel Wheels

3. What did Mick Jagger think of the grunge band Nirvana?

   a. He loved them
   b. He said they sounded like the Stones
   c. He couldn't even remember Kurt Cobain's name
   d. He said they were too angsty

4. What did Keith Richards think of the grunge band Nirvana?

   a. He loved them
   b. He said they sounded like the Stones
   c. He couldn't even remember Kurt Cobain's name
   d. He said they were too angsty

5. Which of these bands opened for the band on their Steel Wheels Tour?

    a. ZZ Top
    b. Guns N' Roses
    c. Metallica
    d. Aerosmith

6. Which of these studio tracks was released on the mostly live album *Flashpoint*?

    a. "Sex Drive"
    b. "Sad Sad Sad"
    c. "Thief in the Night"
    d. "Brand New Car"

7. In 1993, Daryl Jones became the regular bassist for the band. His CV was incredibly impressive. Which of these artists DIDN'T have the privilege of having Daryl play on one of their albums?

    a. Miles Davis
    b. Sting
    c. Neil Young
    d. Elton John

8. What kind of album was the 1994 release *Voodoo Lounge*?

    a. Return to the classic Stones formula
    b. A continuation of their 80s style
    c. An attempt to fit in with grunge
    d. An eclectic world music-oriented album

9. What was *Voodoo Lounge* named after?

    a. A drug
    b. A bar
    c. A cat

d. A car

10. Which of these bands DIDN'T warm up the Stones on their Voodoo Lounge tour?

    a. The Red Hot Chilli Peppers
    b. Counting Crowes
    c. Toad the Wet Sprocket
    d. Stone Temple Pilots

11. Which Stones song did U2 record as the B-side of their 1992 single "Who's Gonna Ride Your Wild Horse?"

    a. "Wild Horses"
    b. "Paint it Black"
    c. "The Spider and the Fly"
    d. "Tumblin Dice"

12. In 1994, the band played the MTV Music Awards. They played "Love is Strong," and one of their classics. Which older song did they perform?

    a. Wild Horses
    b. Angie
    c. Start Me Up
    d. Miss You

13. True or False: In 1994, the Rolling Stones became the first major band to broadcast a show on the internet?

14. The 1995 album Stripped was an unplugged album featuring reworkings of original Stones songs and a cover of Bob Dylan's "Like a Rolling Stone." Who wrote the only other cover song on the album?

    a. Muddy Waters
    b. Howlin' Wolf
    c. Freddie King

d. Willie Dixon

15. The album *Bridges to Babylon* was recorded in Los Angeles, after several records made in all sorts of tropical islands. In which LA studio did they do the bulk of their recordings for the album?

   a. Sunset Sound
   b. Ocean Way Recording
   c. Paramount Recording
   d. Union Recording Studio

16. What actress can be seen in the music video for the song "Anybody Seen My Baby?"

   a. Julia Roberts
   b. Angelina Jolie
   c. Meryl Streep
   d. Susan Sarandon

17. In the song "Saint of Me," Jagger compares himself to several saints. Which saint is not mentioned in the song?

   a. John the Baptist
   b. St. Augustine
   c. St. Paul
   d. St. Patrick

18. Which of these acts DIDN'T support the Stones on the Bridges to Babylon tour?

   a. Bob Dylan
   b. Pearl Jam
   c. Radiohead
   d. Foo Fighters

19. The biggest show on the Bridges to Babylon tour had an attendance of 271,766 people. Where was it held?

    a. River Plate Stadium, Buenos Aires

    b. Amsterdam Arena, Amsterdam

    c. Tokyo Dome, Tokyo

    d. Soldier Field, Chicago

20. The Bridges to Babylon tour was a big success. However, critics accused them of ripping off which other big band with the concept for the tour?

    a. U2

    b. Radiohead

    c. Pearl Jam

    d. Smashing Pumpkins

ANSWERS

1. D- *Steel Wheels*

2. C- Voodoo Lounge

3. D- He said they were too angsty — the full quote: "I'm not in love with [rock music] at the moment. I was never crazy about Nirvana — too angst-ridden for me. I like Pearl Jam. I prefer them to a lot of other bands."

4. C- He couldn't even remember Kurt Cobain's name

5. B- Guns N' Roses

6. A- "Sex Drive"

7. D- Elton John

8. A- Return to the classic Stones formula. However, Jagger was unhappy with it and wanted a more experimental world music kind of album.

9. C- A cat. Richards adopted a cat in Barbados, and the terrace where it liked to sunbathe was Voodo's lounge.

10. C- Toad the Wet Sprocket

11. B- "Paint it Black"

12. C- Start Me Up

13. True

14. D- Willie Dixon

15. B- Ocean Way Recording

16. B- Angelina Jolie

17. D- St. Patrick

18. C- Radiohead

19. A- River Plate Stadium, Buenos Aires

20. A- U2

DID YOU KNOW?

- The Stones signed with Virgin Records in 1992. The head of the label, eccentric millionaire Richard Branson, said that he wasobsessed with the Stones, and it was his lifelong dream to sign them. In 1972, Virgin Records first attempted to sign the Stones with an offer of $3 million. Richards would later release his two solo albums on Virgin. When Branston signed them in 1992, he thought they had a good ten years left in them yet. The millionaire later recalled, "even that guess has proved to underestimate Mick and co.'s longevity. We worked out a deal that gave us rights to their formidable back catalog and released their fantastic album Voodoo Lounge. At the signing party above Mossiman's restaurant, I couldn't stop grinning, and Mick looked pretty pleased, too."

- *Jump Back* was the first Stones compilation released in the CD era and constituted their first release for Virgin Records. It was seen by many as confirmation of the rumors that the main reason the Stones got that big deal from Virgin was that it included the rights to their back catalog.

- Don Was and Jagger clashed during the recording of *Voodoo Lounge*. Don Was specialized in bringing out the best in veteran acts, which often involves bringing out their classic sound elements. Jagger was upset that the album took that direction and told Rolling Stone magazine: "... there were a lot of things that we wrote for *Voodoo Lounge* that Don steered us away from groove songs, African influences, and things like that. And he steered us very clear of all that. And I think it was a mistake." Was fired back that he isn't "anti-groove, just anti-groove without substance, in the context of this album. They had a number of great grooves. But it was like, 'OK, what goes on top of it? Where does it go?' I just felt that it's not what people were looking for from the Stones. I was looking for a sign that they can get real serious about this, still play better than anybody, and write better than anybody." The rift didn't last, and the band rehired Was to work on their reissues of *Some Girls* and *Exile on Main Street*.

- The Verve scored one of the biggest hits of the late 90s with the song "Bittersweet Symphony," released in 1997. The band agreed with the Stones that they could use five notes from the song "The Last Time" to provide the Stones with 50% royalties. However, after the song came out, Jagger and Richards claimed that they used more of the song than the agreement allowed. They correspondingly received all of the royalties. In 2019, the Stones decided to relinquish their rights and writing credits and hand the song back to Verve's frontman, Richard Ashcroft.

- Bob Dylan's song "Like a Rolling Stone" was picked by Rolling Stone magazine as the greatest rock song of the time. Despite a popular association with the Stones, Dylan insisted the name similarities were a pure coincidence, and the song was inspired by the saying "a rolling stone gathers no moss." In 1995, the Stones released a cover of the song as the single from their album *Stripped*. More than once, rumors circulated that Dylan and the Stones would perform the song together. In January 1998, the two acts played Madison Square Garden. However, despite rumors that a guest appearance was in the works, it never happened. Later that year, in Rio de Janeiro, the duet finally happened and was broadcasted live.

CHAPTER 8:

ELDERLY STATESMEN OF ROCK IN THE 21ST CENTURY

1. The Rolling Stones released the compilation *Forty Licks* in 2002. It was the first Stones compilation to do what?

    a. Contain new tracks
    b. Reach #1 on the charts
    c. Include "Honkey Tonk Woman"
    d. Include material from their entire career

2. In 2003, the band played a benefit in Toronto. What was it for?

    a. People with AIDS
    b. SARS victims
    c. Sex trafficking victims
    d. Helping the homeless

3. In 2003, some chains (including the now-defunct Circuit City) pulled all Stones albums and DVDs from their shelves. Why?

    a. Profanity in Stones songs
    b. Misogynistic lyrics
    c. Poor sales
    d. A Stones exclusive deal with another chain

4. The video for the song "Streets of Love" was shot in the Zaphod Beeblebrox club, located in what city in Canada?

a. Vancouver

b. Ottawa

c. Calgary

d. Montreal

5. Who directed the concert film *Shine a Light*, released in 2008?

a. Peter Jackson

b. Steven Spielberg

c. Martin Scorsese

d. Cameron Crowe

6. True or False: Rolling Stone chose *A Bigger Bang* as the album of the year for 2005?

7. In 2006, the A Bigger Bang tour was declared the most profitable of all time. However, other bands have overtaken the record since then. Which of these acts did NOT earn more than the Stones did on that tour?

a. Coldplay

b. Ed Sheeran

c. Guns N' Roses

d. U2

8. Which legendary music executive fell at a Stones show at the Beacon Theater in 2006 and later died of their injuries?

a. Ahmet Ertegun

b. Berry Gordy

c. Malcolm McLaren

d. Keith Altham

9. The band played the Superbowl half-time show in 2006. Which of these songs was NOT played at that show?

a. "(I Can't Get No) Satisfaction"

b. "Rough Justice"

c. "Brown Sugar"

d. "Start Me Up"

10. In 2007, the Stones headlined their first festival in 30 years. What festival did they play?

    a. Glastonbury

    b. Isle of Wight

    c. Rock in Rio

    d. Coachella

11. In 2008, Paramount released *Shine a Light*, a Stones concert film. What was the working budget for the movie?

    a. $500,000

    b. $1,000,000

    c. $1,500,000

    d. $2,000,000

12. In 2010 the band released a remastered version of *Exile on Main Street*. Which song did they release as a single?

    a. Tumbling Dice

    b. Shine a Light

    c. Following the River

    d. Plundered My Soul

13. How many movies did the Stones release in the years 2008-2012?

    a. Two

    b. Three

    c. Four

    d. Five

14. In 2013, the Stones played Hyde Park again, the scene of one of their most famous shows in 1969. What was the same in both shows?

    a. The clothes
    b. The setlist
    c. The price of the tickets
    d. The instruments

15. In 2012, the movie *Crossfire Hurricane* was released. How was it structured?

    a. It was a concert film
    b. It was an interview film
    c. It was an archival footage film
    d. It had interviews with archival footage

16. In 2012, the Stones marked 50 years since their first concert. Where did they play the commemorative show?

    a. The Crawdaddy
    b. The Marquee
    c. Hyde Park
    d. Madison Square Garden

17. In 2016, the Stones played in Cuba for the first time. However, the show had to be delayed. Why?

    a. Richards was injured
    b. Fidel Castro's health deteriorated
    c. President Obama was scheduled to visit
    d. There was a tropical hurricane

18. In 2016, the Stones released their first album in 11 years. How long did it take to record?

    a. One day
    b. Three days

c. A week

d. A month

19. In December 2017, the band released the album *On Air*. What was it?

a. A live album

b. A collection of BBC radio outtakes

c. A new studio album

d. A greatest hits compilation

20. What was the Stones single "Living in a Ghost Town" about?

a. The Chernobyl disaster

b. COVID-19

c. Hiroshima

d. Personal Heartbreak

ANSWERS

1. D- Included material from their entire career. The 1960s Stones music belonged to ABKCO Records, and Virgin owned their later work. *Forty Licks'* first album comprised of the ABKO material and the second consisted of later music.

2. B- SARS victims.

3. D- A Stones exclusive deal with another chain. The band signed an agreement to sell their live DVD *Four Flicks* exclusively at Best Buy.

4. B- Ottawa

5. C- Martin Scorsese

6. False. Unfortunately, they decided it was second best to Kanye West's *Late Registration* album.

7. A- Coldplay. Yes, Ed Sheeran has the number one earning tour of all time as of early 2021.

8. A- Ahmet Ertegun. While Led Zeppelin reunited for a tribute show in Ertegun's honor, the Stones did not show up. However, they dedicated the concert film *Shine a Light* to his memory.

9. C- Brown Sugar

10. B- Isle of Wight

11. B- $1,000,000

12. D- Plundered My Soul

13. D-Five: *Shine a Light; Stones in Exile; Ladies and Gentlemen: The Rolling Stones; The Rolling Stones: Some Girls Live in Texas '78; Crossfire Hurricane.*

14. B. The setlist. Unfortunately, the 2013 concert wasn't free like the first one.

15. D- It had interviews with archival footage

16. B- The Marquee

17. C- President Obama was scheduled to visit

18. B- Three days

19. B- A collection of BBC radio outtakes

20. B- COVID-19

DID YOU KNOW?

- All proceeds from the show at the Beacon Theater, filmed for the *Shine a Light* concert film, went to the Clinton Foundation. Therefore, Hillary and Bill Clinton were in the audience that night. Jagger greeted them by saying to the crowd, "I'd like to welcome President Clinton–and I see she's brought her husband." Clinton is friends with the band and introduced their 2003 free concert in Los Angeles, which was held to support a non-profit group fighting for cleaner air.

- The Stones launched the 50 & Counting tour to commemorate an amazing 50 years of performing as a group. It was somewhat smaller than their usual tours but featured many special guests. Bruce Springsteen, Lady Gaga, Katy Perry, Taylor Swift, and John Mayer all played with the band, among others. However, hardcore fans were most excited to see them play with Mick Taylor again on several gigs.

- In 2014, the Stones played their first, and so far only, show in Israel as part of their 14 On Fire tour's Middle East leg. The band was subjected to pressure by pro-Palestinian groups and rock stars such as Roger Waters, formerly of Pink Floyd, to cancel the show. However, they persisted. The Stones played on the Jewish holiday of Shavuot and, after receiving requests, started the show late to allow religious fans to attend. Israeli promoters tried to get the Stones to play in the country for years, and the band reportedly made $6.7 million just for the one show at Park

Hayarkon. Over 50,000 fans attended the show, creating traffic jams all around Tel Aviv.

- The film *Olé Olé Olé!: A Trip Across Latin America* documented the amazing love local fans have for the band. Perhaps the most remarkable group of fans are the Argentines known as the Rolingas. They are an urban tribe of fanatical Stones fans and bands heavily influenced by them. In 1982, a war broke out between Argentina and the United Kingdom over the sparsely populated Falkland Islands. The military dictatorship running Argentina at that time banned all English music. This inspired resistance centered around fanatical devotion to the Stones, and thus the Rolingas were born. In 2004, a fire broke out at Rolinga band Callejero's show, killing 194 people and injuring over 1,000. However, a decline in Rolinga popularity has occurred in recent years.

- The album *Blue & Lonesome* consisted only of blues covers. Jagger focused heavily on his harmonica playing, and Eric Clapton was drafted for some of the lead guitar work. The covers saw the band coming full circle to their original inspirations, such as Howlin' Wolf and Willie Dixon.

CHAPTER 9:

PERSONAL LIVES, SCANDALS, AND RUMOURS

1. The young Richards was thrown out of the Boy Scouts. What was the reason?

    a. Fighting
    b. Alcohol
    c. Drugs
    d. Girls

2. For years a false rumor circulated that when the police raided the home of Keith Richards, they discovered Jagger eating what out of an intimate part of Marianne Faithful's body?

    a. A banana
    b. Ice cream
    c. Strawberries and cream
    d. A Mars Bar

3. English model Jean Shrimpton was pretty close to the band at one point. Which of these members DIDN'T have a fling or relationship with her?

    a. Bill Wyman
    b. Mick Jagger
    c. Keith Richards
    d. Brian Jones

4. What were the members of the band really doing when the police arrived at Keith Richards' home?

    a. Playing monopoly
    b. Tripping on acid
    c. Having a fistfight
    d. Putting on a play

5. In 1967-68, Richards took a lot of psychedelic drugs. Which rock superstar did he take on a two-to-three day-long acid trip?

    a. Eric Clapton
    b. John Lennon
    c. Jimi Hendrix
    d. Jim Morrison

6. Mick Jagger's girlfriend and famed singer Marianne Faithful had a one-night stand with Richards while she was still with Jagger. How did she describe that night?

    a. Kind of boring
    b. An insane experience
    c. One of the best nights of her life
    d. Terrifying and regretful

7. In 1970, Mick Jagger had a baby with former *Hair* star Marsha Hunt. What kind of father was he to his first child?

    a. He was a loving father
    b. He denied paternity for years
    c. He was distant but dutiful
    d. He was abusive

8. Marsha Hunt had an affair with Mick Jagger. Which other glamorous 1970s rock star had a relationship with her?

a. Marc Bolan
b. David Bowie
c. Robert Plant
d. Greg Allman

9. Who is said to have passed out wearing a Nazi uniform at Mick Jagger's wedding with Bianca Jagger?

a. Keith Moon
b. Ringo Starr
c. David Bowie
d. Keith Richards

10. Who is said to have run entirely naked, aside from a pair of novelty eyeglasses, into Mick and Bianca's honeymoon suite?

a. Keith Moon
b. Ringo Starr
c. David Bowie
d. Keith Richards

11. In which famous spot did Richards accidentally set a fire in the 1970s?

a. Studio 54
b. CBGB's
c. The Apollo Theater
d. The Playboy Mansion

12. In 1973, Richards spent a week living in suburban Melbourne, Australia. What did he do with his free time?

a. Painting
b. Writing
c. Babysitting

d. Knitting

13. On their first tour together, the Tour of the Americas, Wood, and Richards did a lot of cocaine. What was their rule for sharing their stash?

    a. One city, one ounce
    b. One song, one bump
    c. One girl, one line
    d. No snorting during shows

14. According to David Bowie's former bodyguard, Bowie and Jagger took a young girl into the closet for 20 intimate moments. Which celebrity tried to join them but was rebuffed by the bodyguard?

    a. Iggy Pop
    b. Robert Redford
    c. Rudolph Nureyev
    d. Andy Warhol

15. Does Mick Jagger change nappies?

    a. He never did, even for his kids
    b. He did but grudgingly
    c. He enjoys it and even has for bandmates kids
    d. Only for his grandkids

16. In 1976, Keith Richards was arrested in England. What was the reason behind his apprehension?

    a. Drugs with his son in the car
    b. Crashing the car with his son inside
    c. Drinking with his son in the car
    d. Speeding with his son in the car

17. How old was Bill Wyman when he married 18-year-old Mandy Smith?

    a. 32
    b. 42
    c. 52
    d. 62

18. When Jagger met his future wife Jerry Hall, which art rock star was she engaged to?

    a. Bob Geldof
    b. Bryan Ferry
    c. David Byrne
    d. Todd Rundgren

19. Keith Richards claimed that in 2007, he snorted something unusual. What was it?

    a. A line of ants
    b. Condoms
    c. His father's ashes
    d. French fries

20. Does Richards still drink?

    a. He has given it up
    b. He still gets very drunk
    c. Only wine
    d. Only wine and beer

ANSWERS

1. D- Girls. He also says he smuggled whisky into a jamboree, but Richards wasn't caught.

2. D- A Mars bar

3. A- Bill Wyman

4. B- Tripping on acid

5. B- John Lennon. Neither of them could remember what happened on that trip.

6. C- One of the best nights of her life

7. B- He denied paternity for years

8. A- Marc Bolan

9. D- Keith Richards

10. A- Keith Moon

11. D- The Playboy Mansion

12. C- Babysitting

13. B- One song, one bump

14. C- Rudolph Nureyev

15. C- He enjoys it and even has for bandmates kids

16. B- Crashing the car with his son in it. A dent remained where Marlon Richards hit the dashboard, as well as the imprint of his bloody hands.

17. C- 52

18. B- Bryan Ferry

19. C- His fathers' ashes. Richards only snorted his dad, but other people have reportedly snorted the other things.

20. D- Only wine and beer. Or, as Richards put it, "I've knocked the hard stuff on the head. I have a little wine with meals and a Guinness or a beer or two, but otherwise, no. It's like heroin – the experiment is over."

DID YOU KNOW?

1. Richards was once punched in the face by one of his biggest heroes, Chuck Berry. Richards told Jimmy Fallon that he began to play Berry's guitar without permission, the rock'n'roll legend came in yelling "nobody touches my guitar" and punched the British musician. Hard. Richards joked that it was "one of Chuck's biggest hits."

2. In 2007, Richards fell on his head while on a private island of Fiji. He was flown into Australia to undergo neurological surgery. As the guitarist remembers: "I woke up feeling great. And I said, 'Well, when are you going to start?'" Then the doctor replied, "'It's all done, mate.'"

3. In 2014, Mick Jagger's long-time partner, L'Wren Scott, committed suicide in her Manhattan apartment. The two were together from 2001 and onward. Her decision may have related to lingering depression combined with the financial trouble her business faced. She left her entire estate, worth $9 million, to Jagger. The Stones canceled several shows as Jagger was, by all accounts, utterly devastated.

4. Richards went through a lot of trouble quitting heroin in the late 1970s to save the band. He even divorced his wife Anita Pallenberg, at least partially, because she could not kick the habit. However, in recent years, he has made light of that effort. He continues to smoke cigarettes and, in a 2019 interview, said on quitting smoking: "I have tried. So far, unsuccessfully. Lou Reed claimed nicotine was harder to quit than heroin. It is." He also added: "Quitting heroin is like hell, but it's a short hell. Cigarettes are just always there,

and you've always done it. I just pick 'em up and light 'em up without thinking about it."

5. Of all the Stones members, Charlie Watts has the least scandalous past. He tried to keep away from the drugs and messy sexual adventures as much as he could. However, sometimes the drama sucked him in anyway. Richards described one of the few times Watts lost his cool in his biography. In 1984, Jagger was trying to launch his solo career and seems to have become quite insufferable. Jagger called up Watts' hotel room in Amsterdam at 5 AM and asked, "where is my drummer?" Soon after, there was a knock on the door: "Charlie Watts, Savile Row suit, perfectly dressed, tie, shaved, the whole fucking bit. I could smell the cologne! I opened the door, and he didn't even look at me; he walked straight past me, got hold of Mick, and said, "Never call me your drummer again." Then he hauled him up by the lapels of my jacket and gave him a right hook. Mick fell back onto a silver platter of smoked salmon on the table and began to slide towards the open window and the canal below it." Jagger almost fell in, but Richards caught him at just the right time.

CHAPTER 10:

CHARTS, SALES, AND RECOGNITION

1. What is the last top 10 single the Rolling Stones had in the UK as of 2021?

    a. "Anybody Seen My Baby?"
    b. "Love is Strong"
    c. "Start Me Up"
    d. "Brown Sugar"

2. What was the highest-grossing Rolling Stones tour?

    a. A Bigger Bang
    b. No Filter
    c. Voodoo Lounge
    d. American Tour

3. Only one Stones live album reached the top of the British charts. Which one was it?

    a. *Get Yer Ya-Ya's Out! The Rolling Stones in Concert*
    b. *Love You Live*
    c. *Got Live If You Want It!*
    d. *Live Licks*

4. Which of these albums did not rise to the top of the *Billboard* charts?

    a. *Out of Our Heads*
    b. *Sticky Fingers*

    c. *Black and Blue*

    d. *Let It Bleed*

5. How many Rolling Stones albums have sold over 10 million copies in the United States?

    a. 0

    b. 4

    c. 8

    d. 12

6. Which Stones single was the first to top the *Billboard* charts?

    a. "The Last Time"

    b. "(I Can't Get No) Satisfaction"

    c. "Heart of Stone"

    d. "Get Off My Cloud"

7. As of 2021, which Stones album has sold the most copies globally?

    a. *Some Girls*

    b. *Tattoo You*

    c. *Let It Bleed*

    d. *Sticky Fingers*

8. Which was the last single the Stones placed at the top of the *Billboard* charts?

    a. "Start Me Up"

    b. "(I Can't Get No) Satisfaction"

    c. "Miss You"

    d. "Anybody Seen My Baby?"

9. "Sympathy for the Devil" didn't do very well as a single. Which of these countries is the only one in which it charted?

    a. Japan

b. Australia

c. France

d. Switzerland

10. Where do the Stones rank amongst the best-selling artists in US history?

a. 3rd

b. 7th

c. 13th

d. They don't rank

11. In 2012, *Rolling Stone* magazine ranked the top 500 albums of all time. Which Stones Album had the highest position?

a. *Exile on Main Street*

b. *Aftermath*

c. *Beggars Banquet*

d. *Sticky Fingers*

12. How many albums did the Stones place on the original *Rolling Stone* list?

a. 5

b. 9

c. 11

d. 15

13. In 2020, *Rolling Stone* updated the list. Where can the highest-ranking Stones album be found on this list?

a. 5th

b. 7th

c. 12th

d. 14th

14. How many albums did the Stones place on the renewed *Rolling Stone* list?

    a. 6
    b. 8
    c. 9
    d. 10

15. In their list of the greatest artists of all time, where did *Rolling Stone* place their namesake band, the Rolling Stones?

    a. Second
    b. Fourth
    c. Sixth
    d. Eighth

16. Okay, on to the best song. Where did *Rolling Stone* place their top choice for a Stones song--"(I Can't Get No) Satisfaction"--on their list of all-time greatest songs?

    a. First
    b. Second
    c. Third
    d. Fourth

17. The most streamed Stones song on Spotify wasplayed over 500 million times (as of early 2021). Which song is it?

    a. "Paint it Black"
    b. "(I Can't Get No) Satisfaction"
    c. "Start Me Up"
    d. "Gimme Shelter"

18. The Stones had their first *Billboard* hit with "Not Fade Away." Their latest single on the charts was "Living in a Ghost Town" (as of early 2021). How many years elapsed in between?

a. 43
b. 51
c. 56
d. 60

19. Including all formats, how many album equivalents have the Rolling Stones sold throughout their career?

    a. Under 100 Million
    b. Between 100 and 200 Million
    c. Between 200 and 300 million
    d. Between 300 and 400 million

20. How many songs have the Stones place on the *Billboard* top 100 in their career?

    a. 57
    b. 72
    c. 91
    d. 106

21. How many UK No. 1 hits have the Stones scored?

    a. 5
    b. 8
    c. 10
    d. 13

22. What was the last Stones album to reach No. 1 in the UK?

    a. Goats Head Soup
    b. *A Bigger Bang*
    c. *Some Girls*
    d. Blue & Lonesome

ANSWERS

1. C- *Start Me Up*

2. A- A Bigger Bang

3. A- *Get Yer Ya-Ya's Out! The Rolling Stones in Concert*

4. D- *Let It Bleed*. That masterpiece inexplicably peaked at no. 3 in the United States

5. A- Zero

6. B- "(I Can't Get No) Satisfaction"

7. D- *Sticky Fingers*

8. C- "Miss You"

9. C-France

10. C- 13th

11. A- *Exile on Main Street*. Rolling Stone placed it seventh overall.

12. C- 11

13. D- 14th. *Exile on Main Street* tumbled all the way down from 7th place in the original list.

14. A- 6. The Stones had almost half of their albums removed from the list over those eight years.

15. B- Fourth. In his essay on the band for that issue, E-Street Band guitarist Steven Van Zandt wrote a touching article about what made the band great. He told readers: "*Beggars Banquet, Let It Bleed, Sticky Fingers* and *Exile on Main Street*.

They make up the greatest run of albums in history—and all done in three and a half years." He also wrote that if there is one lesson you can learn from the Stones, it's that "if you stick to your guns, and don't compromise with what's trendy, you're gonna go a long fucking way."

16. C- Third. While we know it doesn't count, number one is Bob Dylan's "Like a Rolling Stone." "Sympathy for the Devil" came in 32nd; "Gimme Shelter" 38th; "You Can't Always Get What You Want" placed 100th; "Honky Tonk Woman" 116th; "Jumpin' Jack Flash" 124th; "Paint It Black" 174th; "Street Fighting Man" 295th; "Ruby Tuesday" 303rd; "Wild Horses" 334th; "Tumbling Dice" 424th; "Beast of Burden" 435th; and finally, "Miss You" at 496th.

17. A- "Paint It Black." The answers are in order of popularity if you're curious.

18. C- 56

19. C- Between 200 and 300 million

20. A- 57

21. B- Eight

22. A- *Goats Head Soup*. It's a bit of a tricky question because the remaster reached number one in September 2020. The original release also reached No. 1 back in 1973. The Stones have scored a remarkable 13 No. 1 albums in their home country.

DID YOU KNOW?

- The Grammy Hall of Fame has honored the Rolling Stones by inducting several of their songs and albums. The albums inducted are *Beggars Banquet*, *Exile on Main Street*, *Sticky Fingers*, and *Let it Bleed*. The singles placed are "Paint it Black" and "(I Can't Get No) Satisfaction."

- The Rolling Stones are the eighth best-selling artist in the history of the United States. Interestingly, their highest selling release in the country is not an album at all. Their compilation *Hot Rocks 1964-1971* is their biggest seller. This fact probably does not suit the band since they do not own the rights to that music.

- The 2019 issue of *Billboard* featured their list of the top artists of all time. They rated all acts by crossing the success of singles with albums. Amazingly enough, the two top acts on their list were the Beatles and the Rolling Stones. It truly is the rivalry that will never die. The Beatles beat our boys out on most metrics and took the first spot, while the Stones settled for second. The Fab Four have twenty No. 1 singles in the US to eight by the Stones.

- Meanwhile, the Beatles had nineteen No. 1 albums to nine by the Stones. However, the Stones hold the record with thirty-seven. The two great English bands were followed by (in order): Elton John, Mariah Carey, Madonna, Barbara Streisand, Michael Jackson, Taylor Swift, Stevie Wonder, and Chicago.

- In 1988, Jagger inducted the Beatles into the Hall of Fame. Jagger acknowledged the debt the Stones owed the Beatles.

As he explained, "we were very grateful for that 'cause that really broke us in England. The example of the way they wrote and the original way that they crafted their songs wasn't lost on us. And later on, their success in America broke down many doors that helped everyone else from England that followed. And I thank them very much for all those things." Mick acknowledged the rivalry between the bands, which was always friendly: "We had a lot of rivalry in those early years, and a little bit of friction, but we always ended up friends. I like to think we still are, 'cause they were some of the greatest times of our lives, and I'm proud to be the one that leads them into the Rock and Roll Hall of Fame."

- The Rolling Stones were inducted into the Rock'n'roll Hall of Fame in 1989 by the Who guitarist Pete Townshend. They were honored along with Stevie Wonder, Otis Redding, Dion, and Bessie Smith. *Vulture.com* rated all Hall of Fame inductees from best to worst in an amusing feature, placing the Stones in the scandalously low 15th place. Chuck Berry came in first. Who ranked last at 221st of all the acts? Bon Jovi.

CHAPTER 11:

AWARDS AND NOMINATIONS

1. When did the Stones receive a Grammy for Lifetime Achievement?

    a. 1975
    b. 1986
    c. 2000
    d. They never got one.

2. How many Grammys did the Stones win in the 60s and 70s?

    a. None
    b. Three
    c. Seven
    d. Ten

3. How many times have the Stones won the Grammy for best rock album?

    a. They never won it
    b. Once
    c. Twice
    d. Three times

4. The Grammys first gave out the best album award in 1959. How many times were the Stones nominated for it?

    a. Never
    b. Once
    c. Twice
    d. Five times

5. How many Grammys has the band won overall?

   a. Two
   b. Four
   c. Six
   d. Eight

6. How many *Billboard* awards have the Stones been nominated for?

   a. 10
   b. 15
   c. 20
   d. 25

7. How many *Billboard* awards did the Stones win?

   a. None
   b. One
   c. Five
   d. Eight

8. In 1977, the British Phonographic Industry began to give out its annual popular music awards, nicknamed the BRIT awards. How many BRIT awards have the Stones won over the years?

   a. None
   b. Five
   c. Ten
   d. Fifteen

9. The band was nominated six times for the Echo awards presented by the Deutsche Phono-Akademie. How many times did they win?

   a. Zero

b. Once

c. Twice

d. Three times

10. The video for "Love is Strong" was nominated for three *MTV* Music Awards in 1995. How many did the Stones take home?

   a. None

   b. One

   c. Two

   d. Three

11. The British magazine *New Musical Express*, better known as *NME*, has been giving out musical awards since 1953. How many times were the Stones nominated?

   a. 5

   b. 8

   c. 14

   d. 17

12. The band won the *NME* award for best R&B group for three years straight and then never won it again. In what years did it receive this award?

   a. 1964-1966

   b. 1966-1968

   c. 1968-1970

   d. 1970-1972

13. One of the bands' many films won an *NME* award for Best Music Film. Which one was it?

   a. *The Rolling Stones: Havana Moon*

   b. *Shine a Light*

    c. *Crossfire Hurricane*

    d. *Gimme Shelter*

14. When did Mick Jagger first appear on stage at the Grammy awards?

    a. 1972

    b. 1986

    c. 1995

    d. 2011

15. In 2002, Mick was offered a knighthood by the British Crown. How did he respond?

    a. He refused it

    b. He gladly accepted

    c. He did not reply

    d. He accepted it to honor his father.

16. When did the Rolling Stones receive a star on the Hollywood Walk of Fame?

    a. 1988

    b. 1997

    c. 2010

    d. They never got one

17. Mick Jagger has won a Golden Globe. What was it for?

    a. The use of Stones songs in movie soundtracks

    b. An acting cameo

    c. The use of a Jagger solo song in a soundtrack

    d. His score for a movie

18. Jagger won his first solo award in 1964. What was it?

    a. An *NME* award

    b. A Grammy

c. A Tony

d. An Ivor Novello Award

19. Jagger and Richards were awarded a well-deserved Ivor Novello Special Award for Songwriting. In what year did the British Academy of Songwriters, Composers, and Authors bestow this honor upon them?

a. 1981

b. 1993

c. 2005

d. 2016

20. When were Jagger and Richards inducted into the Songwriters Hall of Fame?

a. 1982

b. 1993

c. 2009

d. They were never inducted

21. Which of these movies included the Stones in their soundtrack and won the Best Picture Academy Award?

a. The Departed

b. Apocalypse Now

c. Goodfellas

d. Full Metal Jacket

ANSWERS

1. B- 1986

2. A- None

3. B- Once. To be fair, they only started giving them out in 1995.

4. B- Once

5. B- Four. They won the Grammy Lifetime Achievement Award in 1987. Best Album for *Voodoo Lounge* and Best Music Video Short Form for "Love is Strong" in 1995. Best Traditional Blues Album for *Blue & Lonesome* in 2018.

6. A- 10

7. B- One. Yes. Once. For *Some Girls*.

8. A- None. Robbie Williams has won 18.

9. A- Zero

10. C- Two. It looks like *MTV* has better taste than most award givers!

11. D- 17

12. B. 1966-1968

13. C- Crossfire Hurricane

14. D- 2011. Though the Stones won the Lifetime Achievement Award in 1986, they accepted the award by video. In 2011, Jagger appeared to pay tribute to soul great Solomon Burke, performing "Everybody Needs Somebody to Love."

15. D- He accepted it to honor his father. Jagger insisted that while the award meant very little to him, it meant the world to his father. In fact, the singer brought along his 92-year-old father to the ceremony. Richards was not happy. The guitarist said, "It sent out the wrong message. It's not what the Stones is about, is it? I thought it was ludicrous to take one of those gongs from the establishment when they did their very best to throw us in jail."

16. D- They never got one. It appears that they never bothered to campaign for one, rather than because the Hollywood Chamber of Commerce is against it.

17. C- The use of a Jagger solo song in a soundtrack. The song was "Old Habits Die Hard," which he recorded for the 2004 movie *Alfie*.

18. A- An *NME* award. Jagger won the award for best New Disc Singer.

19. C- 2005

20. B- 1993

21. A- *The Departed*. "Gimme Shelter" is used in the background as Jack Nicholson gives one of those signature Scorsese voiceover narrations.

DID YOU KNOW?

- Sure, the Stones never won the BRIT awards or performed there. But at least they were involved somehow; in 2000, Ronnie Wood presented Best Soundtrack's award alongside actress Thora Birch. Intoxicated DJ Brandon Block was pranked into believing that he had won a prize, and he stepped onto the stage. Wood and Block traded several insults and were separated by security. Wood then threw a drink in Block's face. Ronnie Wood made headlines once again when he traveled to the 2020 BRIT awards using the Tube (what Londoners call the London Underground system). Video of him engaging fans in a friendly manner went viral.

- As you could see from the questions, the Recording Academy did not exactly embrace the Rolling Stones. When asked why the Academy ignored him for so long, Jagger told a newscaster, "I don't really know or care. I think all these award shows should be taken off the air." He even insisted, "I didn't want to accept this award, but the rest of the group wanted it, so I went along with it." Jagger couldn't hold his resentment even when accepting the award (via videolink) and said, "the joke is on you." However, Richards was more positive and said, "maybe we can pick up a second-lifetime achievement award in another 20 years."

- Richards was nominated for a Spike Award for Best Celebrity Cameo for this appearance as Captain Teague in Pirates of the Caribbean: At World's End. The guitarist played the father of Jack Sparrow, the character played by

Johnny Depp. The casting was an inside joke, as Depp had often noted that he based the Sparrow character's mannerisms on Richards. The role was so well received that Richards reprised it in the subsequent release Pirates of the Caribbean: On Stranger Tides. Spike TV later awarded Richards with Rock Immortal Award.

- The Rolling Stones continue to see themselves as outsiders in the music business. That is why Richards and Wyman have both served as judges for the Independent Music Awards. They have both stated that they prefer to be associated with more minor acts trying to do their thing than with the mainstream music establishment.

- Richards picked up the Q Magazine Special Merit Award in 2015. The awards are handed out at 2 PM, requiring Richards to get up early, by his standards. He told reporters at the ceremony that this allowed him to engage in an activity he does not often enjoy: "I love this breakfast thing. It's a novelty to me."

CHAPTER 12:

FORMER MEMBERS, SIDEMEN AND HIRED GUNS

1. Why was pianist Ian Stewart removed from the original
    Rolling Stones lineup in 1963?

    a. The band didn't require much piano work
    b. Creative differences
    c. Stewart didn't look right
    d. Personal disagreements

2. What was the last album long-time collaborator Ian Stewart
    played on before passing away from a heart attack?

    a. *Undercover*
    b. *Tattoo You*
    c. *Dirty Work*
    d. *Steel Wheels*

3. What other legendary band did Ian Stewart play with?

    a. The Beatles
    b. The Who
    c. Led Zeppelin
    d. The Kinks

4. Ian Stewart started a band with Charlie Watts in the late
    1970s. What was it called?

    a. Rocket 88
    b. The Beat

c. Crispy Ambulance

d. The Flowerpots

5. Which former member of the Allman Brothers Band is a long-time member of the Stones touring band and a regular contributor to their albums?

a. Dicky Betts

b. Butch Trucks

c. Chuck Leavell

d. Jaimoe

6. Which song on the 1991 live album *Flashpoint* featured an Eric Clapton solo?

a. "Factory Girl"

b. "Little Red Rooster"

c. "Paint It Black"

d. "Brown Sugar"

7. Noted R&B artist and producer Babyface worked with the band on a track off *Bridges to Babylon*. However, his contribution was discarded. Which track was it?

a. "Already Over Me"

b. "Gunface"

c. "Out of Control"

d. "Saint of Me"

8. In what year did Mick Taylor last play on a Stones studio song?

a. 1975

b. 1987

c. 1993

d. 2009

9. Which of these classic albums features Mick Taylor's guitar work?

    a. "Waiting for Columbus" by Little Feat
    b. "Bad Company by Bad" Company
    c. "Blood on the Tracks" by Bob Dylan
    d. "Rising for the Moon" by Fairport Convention

10. In 2007, Mick Taylor toured the East Coast, playing songs by which legendary guitarist?

    a. Eric Clapton
    b. Stevie Ray Vaughn
    c. Duane Allman
    d. Jimi Hendrix

11. Billy Preston was unfairly blamed for some of the mediocre albums the Stones released in the late 70s. However, he played on many of their classic albums as well. Which of these albums DIDN'T feature Preston?

    a. *Goat's Head Soup*
    b. *Exile on Main Street*
    c. *Let it Bleed*
    d. *Sticky Fingers*

12. Billy Preston played on three No. 1 *Billboard* hit singles. Which of these is not one of them?

    a. "Angie"
    b. "Get Back"
    c. "Will It Go Round in Circles"
    d. "Nothing from Nothing"

13. Backing vocalist Lisa Fischer played with the Stones for over twenty years. Which of these acts did Lisa NOT sing backing vocals for?

a. Luther Vandross
b. Nine Inch Nails
c. The Foo Fighters
d. Tina Turner

14. Lisa Fischer won the 1992 Grammy Award for Best Female R&B Vocal Performance for her performance on which hit single?

    a. "Save Me"
    b. "So Intense"
    c. "How Can I Ease the Pain"
    d. "Colors of Love"

15. In her first job as a background vocalist, Merry Clayton of "Gimme Shelter" fame sang in support of which legendary artist?

    a. Marvin Gaye
    b. Ray Charles
    c. Otis Redding
    d. Wilson Pickett

16. Which other essential classic rock song did Merry Clayton sing backup vocals on?

    a. "Sweet Home Alabama" by Lynyrd Skynyrd
    b. "Hotel California" by the Eagles
    c. "Money" by Pink Floyd
    d. "Proud Mary" by Creedence Clearwater Revival

17. Bobby Keys played the saxophone on several Stones classics. Which of these songs features his playing?

    a. "Miss You"
    b. "Slave"
    c. "Can't You Hear Me Knocking"

d. "Neighbors"

18. Wayne Shorter, one of the most gifted jazz saxophonists of his generation, plays on which Stones song?

    a. "How Can I Stop"
    b. "Casino Boogie"
    c. "Emotional Rescue"
    d. "Live with Me"

19. In 1973, Bobby Keys missed a Stones show in Belgium. What was he doing instead?

    a. He was in the hospital
    b. He was playing with a local jazz band
    c. He was drunk in a ditch
    d. He was in a bathtub filled with champagne

20. African percussionist Rocky Dijon played on some of the Stones best albums. Which of these albums DON'T feature his subtle stylings?

    a. *Beggars Banquet*
    b. *Let it Bleed*
    c. *Sticky Fingers*
    d. *Exile on Main Street*

ANSWERS

1. C- Stewart didn't look right. Manager Andrew Loog Oldham said he didn't fit with the 'bad boy' image the band was trying to foster. Therefore, he began to contribute piano as a non-member.

2. A- *Undercover*

3. C- Led Zeppelin. Stewart contributed the wonderful boogie-woogie piano to "Rock and Roll" and "Boogie With Stu," named after the pianists' nickname: Stu.

4. A- Rocket 88

5. C- Chuck Leavell

6. B- "Little Red Rooster"

7. A- "Already Over Me"

8. D- 2009. That year Taylor played the guitar parts for "Plundered My Soul," the single off the remastered version of *Exile on Main Street*.

9. A- "Waiting for Columbus" by Little Feat

10. D- Jimi Hendrix. Taylor toured with the rhythm section of the original Jimi Hendrix Experience: Mitch Mitchell and Billy Cox.

11. C- *Let It Bleed*

12. A- "Angie." "Get Back was a Beatles single. The other two were No. 1 singles played by Preston and written with Bruce Fisher.

13. C- The Foo Fighters

14. C- "How Can I Ease the Pain"

15. B- Ray Charles

16. A- "Sweet Home Alabama" by Lynyrd Skynyrd

17. C- "Can't You Hear Me Knocking"

18. A- "How Can I Stop"

19. D- He was in a bathtub filled with champagne. Bobby was spending time with a young French woman in the tub.

20. D- *Exile on Main Street*

DID YOU KNOW?

- Lisa Fischer has moved on from singing backup and now is the band Grand Baton's lead singer. However, her time working with the Stones has left an indelible mark on her work. Her band reworks rock classics by acts as diverse as the Police, Led Zeppelin, and Robert Palmer. Fischer is thankful for her time with the Stones and says, "They have been so supportive and loving and kind to me. I miss them. I love them to the ends of the Earth."

- Bobby Keys not only played sax on many classic Stones songs, but he also lived the same hard driving rock'n'roll lifestyle as some of its members. He once told Rolling Stone magazine, "I've been smoking pot for over 50 years, and I never let a day go by unless I'm in jail. I am a devout pothead. I have been, will be, don't see a damn thing wrong with it except the cost." Keys met the Stones when he recorded an album with Delaney & Bonnie in 1969 when the Stones made *Let it Bleed* nearby. The band invited Bobby to sit in on the song "Live With Me." Thus, began an association that led to Keys playing sax on several Stones albums. His most notable contributions were on "Brown Sugar" and "Sweet Virginia." Keys and Richards were both born on the same day and became very close friends. When Keys passed away in 2014, Richards released a statement reading, "I have lost the largest pal in the world, and I can't express the sense of sadness I feel, although Bobby would tell me to cheer up."

- As we have already discussed, Merry Clayton was pregnant when she recorded her unforgettable background vocals for

Stones classic "Gimme Shelter." However, the singer could not listen to or perform that song for years because of the tragedy that befell her right after that recording session. The Stones called Clayton in the middle of the night and asked her to participate in the recording. She famously arrived in her curlers but ready to go. Jagger recalled, "We randomly phoned up this poor lady in the middle of the night, and she arrived in her curlers and proceeded to do that in one or two takes, which is pretty amazing. She came in and knocked off this rather odd lyric. It's not the sort of lyric you give anyone–'Rape, murder/It's just a shot away'–but she got into it, as you can hear on the record." Unfortunately, not long after the session was completed, Clayton suffered a miscarriage. It is quite possible that it was caused by her vocals' intensity and the late hours of the session. However, the brilliant vocalist eventually overcame the pain. In 1986, she told a reporter, "That was a dark, dark period for me, but God gave me the strength to overcome it. I turned it around. I took it as life, love, and energy and directed it in another direction, so it doesn't really bother me to sing 'Gimme Shelter' now. Life is short as it is, and I can't live on yesterday."

- Session piano player Nicky Hopkins is one of the unsung heroes of the classic rock era. Starting with his work as a teenager playing for Screaming Lord Sutch and the Savages and up to his death in 1994, Hopkins played on countless rock classics as a session musician. He also played for two (excellent) bands as a full member: the Jeff Beck Group and Quicksilver Messenger Service. Perhaps his most distinctive contribution to the Rolling Stones music was in "She's a Rainbow," which is dominated by his piano playing. His playing on "Beggars Banquet" was exemplary, shining on "Sympathy for the Devil" and "No Expectations." You may also remember his beautiful parts on "Monkey Man," "Loving Cup," "Angie," and "Waiting for a Friend." Other well-known songs with memorable parts by Hopkins include Joe Cocker's "You Are So Beautiful," John Lennon's "Jealous Guy," and the Kinks' "Sunny Afternoon." What a talent.

- Brian Jones was a gifted slide player, and he often complimented Richards' muscular riffs with his elegant refrains. When Jones died, neither Keith nor new recruit Mick Taylor could fill the gap. Therefore, the Stones turned to American guitarist Ry Cooder when they needed expert slide playing. By the time he began playing with the Stones, Ry had earned a solid reputation for his work with Taj Mahal, Randy Newman, and Captain Beefheart. The Stones used him often. You can hear his mandolin playing on "Love in Vain" and the gorgeous slide on "Sister Morphine." However, his most significant contribution to the Stones is probably the riff for "Honky Tonk Woman." Some people believe that Ry wrote it, and if you listen to his solo material, you can see why. The session guitarist also taught Richards the open G tuning, which Richards later used for "Jumpin' Jack Flash," "Gimme Shelter," and "Start Me Up." Ry is so good that Rolling Stone magazine placed him eighth on their list of the greatest guitarists of all time.

CHAPTER 13:

BIG BAND, BIG MONEY

1. In 1981, the Stones signed their first major sponsorship deal. The company got a large number of free tickets and their name plastered on the tickets and merchandise. Which company was it?

    a. Budweiser
    b. Nike
    c. Jovan
    d. Coca Cola

2. What major advertising campaign used the song "Start Me Up" as its main jingle?

    a. Windows 95
    b. Pepsi
    c. Honda
    d. McDonald's

3. Jagger vetoed a musical that would be called *Sympathy for the Devil*. What was the play about?

    a. Satan was rebelling against God
    b. Altamont
    c. Machiavelli
    d. The Church of Satan

4. Where is the Rolling Stones Museum located?

    a. London
    b. Altamont

c. Barbados

d. Slovenia

5. The song that made the Stones the most money was "(I Can't Get No) Satisfaction." Where did Jagger write it?

   a. In his bedroom

   b. In the south of France

   c. By the pool in Tampa

   d. On a plane

6. Who handles selling and claiming royalties for the Richard/Jagger catalog?

   a. Jagger and Richards do it personally

   b. BMG

   c. EMI

   d. ABKCO

7. How much is a first press copy of the Rolling Stones debut album worth if it is in mint condition?

   a. $500

   b. $6,000

   c. $11,000

   d. $122,000

8. What is the price of an average Rolling Stones concert ticket in the 21st Century?

   a. $100

   b. $250

   c. $350

   d. $500

9. How much did the Stones highest-earning tour, the A Bigger Bang Tour, bring in?

a. Over $100 million
b. Over $500 million
c. Over a $750 million
d. Over $1 billion

10. What is the estimated net worth of Keith Richards?

a. Over $200 million
b. Over $300 million
c. Over $500 million
d. Over $750 million

11. What is the estimated net worth of Mick Jagger?

a. Over $200 million
b. Over $300 million
c. Over $500 million
d. Over $750 million

12. Which of these musicians is believed to have a higher net worth than either Jagger or Richards?

a. Jimmy Buffett
b. Roger Waters
c. Eric Clapton
d. Ringo Starr

13. In late 2020, Mick Jagger purchased a ranch in Florida for girlfriend Melania Hamrick. How much did he reportedly pay for it?

a. $1,000,000
b. $1,500,000
c. $2,000,000
d. $2,500,000

14. How does the band currently split its touring and merchandise earnings?

    a. Equally between Wood, Jagger, Richards, Watts, and Darryl Jones

    b. Equally between Wood, Jagger, Richards, and Watts

    c. Equally between Wood, Jagger, Richards, Watts, and Wyman

    d. Jagger and Richards make half, and the rest split it

15. How much did the Rolling Stones earn per night on their No Filter Tour, which ran from September 2017 to June 2019?

    a. $1 Million

    b. $5 Million

    c. $8 Million

    d. $10 Million

16. Who ranked above the Stones in the list of the highest-earning musical acts of 2019?

    a. Ariana Grande

    b. Ariana Grande and Elton John

    c. Ariana Grande, Elton John, and the Jonas Brothers

    d. Nobody, the Stones topped the list

17. Richards and his wife Patti Hansen sold their Penthouse in Manhattan in 2018 at a loss of over $2 million of what they originally paid for it. How much did it go for?

    a. $7.75 million

    b. $9.75 million

    c. $12.75 million

    d. $14.75 million

18. Charlie Watts has a side hustle as a horse breeder on a stud farm in Devon. How much will he charge you for a vial of horse semen?

    a. 1000 British Pounds
    b. 2000 British Pounds
    c. 3000 British Pounds
    d. 4000 British Pounds

19. How much does it cost to use a Stones song for a TV commercial?

    a. $4 Million
    b. $5 Million
    c. $6 Million
    d. $7 Million

20. How much did a Stones concert cost in 1969?

    a. $3-5
    b. $5-8
    c. $10-12
    d. $13-15

ANSWERS

1. C- Jovan

2. A-Windows 95

3. C- Machiavelli

4. D- Slovenia

5. C- By the pool in Tampa

6. B- BMG

7. B- $6,000. One has sold for $6,685,000, to be precise.

8. C- $350. $375, to be exact.

9. B- Over $500 million. $558,255,52 to name an exact figure.

10. B- Over $300 million

11. B- Over $300 million

12. A- Jimmy Buffett. Yup.

13. C- $2,000,000

14. B- Equally between Ronnie, Mick, Keith, Charlie

15. D- $10 Million

16. D- Nobody, the Stones topped the list. They made $65 million to Grande's paltry $44.3 million.

17. B- $9.75 million. $12.75 million was the price they bought it for.

18. B- 2000 British Pounds. This went down from the previous 2600 price, presumably because COVID-19 is slowing down business.

19. A- $4 Million

20. B- $5-8

DID YOU KNOW?

- Bill Wyman is not particularly rich. The Stones made plenty of money before 1993, but they have made the absolute majority of it since their massive tours. So, Wyman's decision to leave the band was a pretty bad decision from a financial standpoint. However, Wyman says he has no regrets. In an interview, he admitted that when he left, "the big money wasn't there yet. I had a small nest egg, and I can live nicely, but I can't rely on Stones royalties to support me. I have to work, and I'm not in the same league as the boys who stayed on. But I wanted to have fun. Playing with the Stones, there was always such a lot of pressure. The next album or single always had to be the best, or at least sell more." To pay the bills, Wyman formed Bill Wyman's Rhythm Kings and continues to tour at age 83.

- As you can see, the Stones are now incredibly good with money. But this was not always the case. Their first manager, Andrew Loog Oldham, was a brilliant publicist but very poor with money decisions. He entrusted the band's contract negotiations with Allen Klein, a man who turned out to be quite disreputable. The Stones sued Klein for withholding royalties and neglecting to pay their taxes for five years. The unscrupulous manager kept the Stones money, and when one of the band members needed to make a purchase, he would loan them their own money back with interest. In 1968, the payments stopped coming. Klein would also go on to screw over the Beatles. He sided with John and Yoko against Paul McCartney and helped drive the Fab Four apart. Despite all the damage Klein had done to legendary British rock groups, Klein kept the royalties for the pre-1971 Stones songs and continued to make money off them for decades. In 2003, he made a lucrative deal with Steve Jobs to make the early Stones hits available on iTunes.

- The Rolling Stones are thought to be the wealthiest rock band in the UK, but probably not globally. Amongst bands that have broken up, there is no question that the Beatles are the richest if you take the estates of the deceased George Harrison and John Lennon into account. Among currently active bands, Metallica is considered the wealthiest. They have amassed a net worth of over $1 billion. Irish rock band U2 is also more affluent, as Bono has double Mick Jagger's net worth.

- Although Jagger is incredibly rich, he still puts his place up for short-term rent when he isn't there, like the rest of us. His home on the privately-owned island of Mustique rents for anywhere between $15,000 and $30,000 a week, depending on the season. The house is Japanese-inspired and contains several self-contained rooms within a beautiful garden. Rental comes with a staff of six, including a butler and a gourmet chef. If you take the deal, tell Jagger we sent you.

- Jagger is plenty prosperous but would have been richer if not for the messy divorce with model Jerry Hall. The relationship ended in 1999 when Jagger impregnated a Brazilian model, displeasing Hall. After a contentious process in which Jagger maintained that the two were not genuinely married under British law, the former couple solved the problem with their dissolution in 1999. Hall used the same divorce lawyer employed by Princess Diana in her divorce from Prince Charles, and she got her money's worth. Jagger reportedly paid a settlement of close to $30 million to the Texan model. Today Hall is married to media mogul Rupert Murdoch who is reportedly worth around $22 billion.

CHAPTER 14:

SOLO CAREERS

1. In 1985, Mick was photographed in drag for the cover of his album, *She's the Boss*. How much money did he spend on his women's clothing?

    a. 5,000 Pounds
    b. 10,000 Pounds
    c. 30,000 Pounds
    d. 50,000 Pounds

2. How well did Mick's first solo album, *She's the Boss*, do in the United States?

    a. It went platinum
    b. It went multi-platinum
    c. It was a gold record
    d. It sold very poorly

3. Who played on the song "Lonely at the Top," which led off the album *She's the Boss*?

    a. Pete Townshend
    b. Jeff Beck
    c. Herbie Hancock
    d. All of the above

4. What did Richards think of *She's the Boss*?

    a. He grudgingly admitted it's good
    b. He hated it
    c. He refused to comment

d. He never listened to it

5. Jagger had a hit single with the song "Just Another Night." However, a reggae artist Patrick Alley sued him for copyright infringement on his piece with the same title. How did the court rule on that case?

    a. Mick lost and was forced to pay Alley
    b. Mick won and didn't have to pay
    c. They settled out of court
    d. Mick voluntarily gave Alley writing credits

6. Mick's second solo album, *Primitive Cool*, didn't do as well as the first album. What was its peak position on the *Billboard* chart?

    a. Didn't break the Hot 100
    b. Didn't break the top 40
    c. Made top 20
    d. Made top 10

7. Jeff Beck played with Jagger on the album *Primitive Cool*. Why didn't he tour with Jagger to promote the album?

    a. Time constraints
    b. The two didn't get along personally
    c. Jagger wanted a visual spectacle
    d. Beck wanted a less commercial sound

8. Jagger toured behind the *Primitive Cool* album. What kind of tour was scheduled?

    a. A massive world tour
    b. A North American tour
    c. An Australian and Japanese tour
    d. A small clubs tour

9. Which A-list producer worked on Jagger's third solo album, *Wandering Spirit*?

    a. Rick Rubin
    b. Don Was
    c. Mutt Lange
    d. Bob Rock

10. Which of these artists DIDN'T co-write songs with Jagger on his 2001 solo release *Goddess in the Doorway*?

    a. Wyclef Jean
    b. Rob Thomas
    c. Beck
    d. Lenny Kravitz

11. In 2007, WEA/Rhino released a compilation called *The Very Best of Mick Jagger*. It included the unreleased song "Too Many Cooks (Spoil the Stew)." Who produced it?

    a. John Lennon
    b. Eric Clapton
    c. Keith Richards
    d. David Bowie

12. Before Richards released his first solo album, *Talk is Cheap*, he had always said that there was only one reason he would ever release a solo album. What was the reason?

    a. The Stones were no longer good
    b. The Stones would not let him express himself
    c. He had sold out
    d. The Stones had broken up

13. After recording *Talk is Cheap*, Keith said his perspective on Jagger had changed. In what way did it change?

a. He respected Jagger less
b. He admired Jagger more
c. He realized he loved Jagger
d. He realized he hated Jagger

14. In 1988, Richards and his band, the X-Pensive Winos, recorded *Live at the Hollywood Palladium*, a well-received live album. Which of these Stones songs was NOT on that album?

    a. "Time Is on My Side"
    b. "Happy"
    c. "Connection"
    d. "Sweet Virginia"

15. Which musical platform released Keith Richards' single "Trouble" as a single to promote its digital musical offerings?

    a. Spotify
    b. iHeart Radio
    c. Pandora
    d. iTunes

16. Ronnie Wood's most successful solo album was 1979's *Gimme Some Neck*. What was its highest position on the *Billboard* album charts?

    a. 89
    b. 73
    c. 41
    d. 23

17. In 1992, Charlie Watts released his first solo album. It was a highly acclaimed tribute to which jazz legend?

a. Max Roach

b. Bill Evans

c. Charlie Parker

d. Charles Mingus

18. On Bill Wyman's solo album, *Stone Alone*, which famous singer plays a saxophone break?

a. Joe Cocker

b. Al Green

c. Chaka Khan

d. Van Morrison

19. Who was the lead guitarist on the *Willie and the Poor Boys* band Bill put together in 1983?

a. Mick Taylor

b. Jimmy Page

c. George Harrison

d. Eric Clapton

20. In 1979, Mick Taylor put out a well-received eponymous solo album debut. Which song on it was recorded by the Stones, but they refused to release it?

a. "Leather Jacket"

b. "Slow Blues"

c. "Baby, I Want You"

d. "Alabama"

ANSWERS

1. C-30,000 Pounds

2. A- It went Platinum

3. D- All of the above. Not an inadequate amount of talent for one song.

4. D- He never listened to it. Even decades later, he insisted that he had never heard it and never intended to.

5. B- Mick won and didn't have to pay. After winning, the singer said, "My reputation is really cleared. If you're well-known, people stand up and take shots at you. It's one of those things in a litigious society."

6. B- Didn't break top 40. It peaked at number 41.

7. C- Jagger wanted a visual spectacle. Jeff was reportedly disappointed that Mick wanted to tour with dancing girls and background singers. He wanted a more stripped-down rock approach.

8. C- An Australian and Japanese tour. He was not confident in the album after the poor reception it had. Some also believe Jagger scheduled the Japanese leg to convince the Japanese to let the Stones in for future tours since they had been banned from the country over past drug arrests. If that was the goal, it worked.

9. A- Rick Rubin. Rubin has produced countless rock and rap classics over the years, including Run-DMC's pathbreaking albums and the Red Hot Chili Pepper's *Blood Sugar Sex Magik*.

10. C- Beck

11. A- John Lennon.

12. D- The Stones had broken up. Richards felt like they basically had broken up when he was working on the album.

13. B- He respected Jagger more. Richards realized how much he depended on Jagger for elements of the recording process that the guitarist had previously taken for granted.

14. D- Sweet Virginia

15. C- iHeart Radio

16. C- 41

17. C- Charlies Parker. The album is called *Tribute to Charlie Parker with Strings*.

18. D- Van Morrison

19. B- Jimmy Page

20. A- "Leather Jacket." It is a beautiful song, and the Stones really should have released it.

DID YOU KNOW?

- The recording of Jagger's debut solo album *She's the Boss* interfered with the recording of the Stones album *Dirty Work*, which took place on the outskirts of Paris at Boulogne-Billancourt. The band had to start sessions without the singer, who was busy shooting the solo album videos. With the leader not particularly committed to that Stones album, other members often neglected to show up to the sessions. Jagger recorded most of the lead vocals, with the other members absent. There was also no tour to support the album.

- Live Aid was a charity concert event staged to help those affected by the 1983-1985 famine in Ethiopia. It was held simultaneously at Wembley Stadium in London and JFK Stadium in Philadelphia. The fight between Jagger and the rest of the band over his solo career was quite evident during the internationally broadcast Live Aid concert. Jagger played a solo set instead of performing with the guys. Adding insult to injury, he played Stones classic "Miss You" on his own and did the solo song "Just Another Night." He then invited star artist Tina Turner on stage, and the two did renditions of Jackson Five's song "State of Shock," and Stones' classic "It's Only Rock 'n' Roll." Their performance was well received, with palpable chemistry between Jackson and Turner. Meanwhile, Richards and Wood were scheduled to play with Bob Dylan at the event. The superstar act was introduced by Hollywood A-lister Jack Nicholson but went quickly downhill from there. The three legends were out of tune and looking worse for wear, as they did violence to the timeless classic "Blowin' in the Wind." Microphones made screeching noises and people wandered on stage during the performance. Needless to say, the success of Jagger's performance and the failure of his bandmates only fueled the divide in the band.

- In support of his album *Gimme Some Neck*, Wood formed a band which he called the New Barbarians. The band included Richards, jazz fusion bassist Stanley Clarke, drummer Joseph Zigaboo of funk band the Meters, Faces keyboard player Ian McLagan and Stones sideman Bobby Keys on sax. The band only played 20 shows together. However, they had one particularly high-profile gig when they opened for Led Zeppelin at the 1979 Knebworth Festival in front of around 200,000 paying customers. The band was billed ahead of veteran acts such as Todd Rundgren, Marshall Tucker, and Fairport Convention. The band also opened for the Stones, most notably in the 1979 concert given to satisfy the terms of Richards' Canadian drug sentence the previous year. In 2006, a New Barbarians live album was released called *Buried Alive: Live in Maryland*.

- Charlie Watts got his start as a jazz drummer, and his solo career consisted almost exclusively of jazz releases. The most interesting release is the Charlie Watts/Jim Keltner project which sees him compose loving tributes to a series of jazz drumming greats: from Art Blakey to Tony Williams. Most listeners would agree that Charlie is genuinely on his element in a jazz setting.

- Wyman was the first member of the band to try his hand at a solo career. He released a series of enjoyable and unpretentious albums throughout the years, most recently in 2015's Back to Basics. He even enjoyed a British top twenty hits in 1981 with the humorous disco song "(Si Si) Je Suis un Rock Star." The song was meant for Ian Dury, but when he couldn't get the singer to listen to it, Wyman recorded the song himself in an accent he described as "cockney French."

Made in the USA
Middletown, DE
01 March 2022

61958930R10076